Museums
Environment
Energy

MUSEUMS & GALLERIES COMMISSION

Museums
Environment
Energy

A publication of the Museums & Galleries Commission
with the support of the Energy Efficiency Office

May Cassar
Editor

LONDON: HMSO

ISBN 0 11 290519 6

British Library Cataloguing in Publication Data
A CIP catalogue record for this book is available from the British Library

HMSO publications are available from:

HMSO Publications Centre
(Mail, fax and telephone orders only)
PO Box 276, London, SW8 5DT
Telephone orders 071-873 9090
General enquiries 071-873 0011
(queuing system in operation for both numbers)
Fax orders 071-873 8200

HMSO Bookshops
49 High Holborn, London, WC1V 6HB
(counter service only)
071-873 0011 Fax 071-831 1326
258 Broad Street, Birmingham, B1 2HE
021-643 3740 Fax 021-643 6510
33 Wine Street, Bristol, BS1 2BQ
0272 264306 Fax 0272 294515
9–21 Princess Street, Manchester, M60 8AS
061-834 7201 Fax 061-833 0634
16 Arthur Street, Belfast, BT1 4GD
0232 238451 Fax 0232 235401
71 Lothian Road, Edinburgh, EH3 9AZ
031-228 4181 Fax 031-229 2734

HMSO's Accredited Agents
(see Yellow Pages)

and through good booksellers

Front cover illustration by Kevin Mansfield

Contents

Foreword

I am delighted to welcome the publication of the proceedings of the highly successful conference on Environmental Control in Museums and Galleries organised jointly by the Museums & Galleries Commission and the Government's Energy Efficiency Office. I am sure that it will prove of value to architects, engineers, building managers, curators and conservators in reducing the costs of heating and lighting museums and galleries in addition to improving the environment in the buildings for both visitors and treasures.

We all have a responsibility to play a role in reducing the emissions of carbon dioxide into the atmosphere and thus help protect the planet from the threat of global warming. The conference showed that establishments such as museums and galleries which bring alive the past, can also play a role in preserving the future.

I commend the lessons and knowledge in this book.

THE EARL OF ARRAN
20 January 1994

1

Introduction

May Cassar

Why *energy efficiency?* What is its relevance to museums? How can saving energy affect the preservation of museum collections? Every day the designers and specifiers of museums are faced with conflicting challenges: to provide a comfortable environment for staff and visitors and also to provide conditions in which the precious contents of cultural buildings will be preserved.

It is inevitable that the protection of museum collections involves some form of environmental control. However, environmental control costs money. While the purchase of monitoring and control equipment can be grant-aided by statutory bodies, including the Department of National Heritage, the Museums & Galleries Commission, The Conservation Unit and Area Museum Councils, running and maintenance costs are usually the responsibility of the museum.

The cost of energy usage by museums, a significant portion of which is spent on environmental control, may not escape close scrutiny when the squeeze on resources tightens. Should national energy savings become necessary, the building manager, the conservator and the curator may need to demonstrate that environmental control has been achieved in the most cost-effective way.

The availability of gas and electricity has meant that over the years solutions to environmental problems have often been energy-intensive, with not enough care being given to energy-efficient features in building design. It should not be forgotten that today's gerry buildings may be tomorrow's heritage, so the question of whether the energy-dependent buildings constructed today can function tomorrow when energy may not be in such plentiful supply, must be addressed.

This publication demonstrates the need for museums to strike a balance between environmental control and energy efficiency. In doing so, it presents both conventional and alternative solutions to refute the argument that saving energy means 'switching off' an appliance, a practice which is unacceptable in museums if they are to fulfil their duty of care of their collections.

The group of papers published here include those by Oreszczyn *et al*, Bordass, Reading, Ascough and Carver which were presented at a conference on *Saving Energy for a Better Environment* in November 1991. Two case-studies on energy-efficiency measures, one on the National Museum of Photography, Film and Television in Bradford and the other on the

Whitby Museum, have been commissioned to illustrate how two museums of different size and scale of operation have succeeded in practice in improving environmental control and energy efficiency. The publication concludes with a list of management priorities for museums wishing to assess their practice in terms of environmental control and energy efficiency.

December 1994

Museum Environments and Energy Efficiency:

Are Our Current Priorities Right?

William T. Bordass MA PhD William Bordass Associates

Introduction

At a conference at the Victoria & Albert Museum in 1984[1], Gael de Guichen of ICCROM observed – and only slightly tongue-in-cheek – that the best way mankind had yet devised to destroy the objects they valued was to put them in museums. Here they would be bombarded with light, surrounded by unsuitable and often poorly controlled air, subjected to vibration, and put collectively at risk from vandalism, theft, fire, flood, and system failure. Having created such hazards by collecting things and putting them on display, we need to use energy – both our own and from purchased fuels – to reduce the consequent risks. But can we be sure that what we are doing is part of the solution, and not compounding the problem: both locally and globally. How can we help to ensure that things are displayed and looked after more effectively and energy efficiently?

I would like to set the scene for the publication while trying to avoid issues which other papers will cover on the technical side, largely air-conditioning and lighting.

Lighting issues are common in one way or other to all museums and galleries: obtaining the best visibility of the objects in their environment while minimising photo-degradation where this is important. Here the strategy is fundamentally a low-energy one: providing the minimum exposure at the lowest levels at which they can be seen reasonably well, though the ways in which natural and artificial light are actually obtained and controlled are often somewhat roundabout and more energy-intensive than they could be! Annual lux-hour standards (preferably frequency-weighted) are now well understood but less easily applied, particularly where some natural light is required.

On the other hand, only relatively few museums and galleries in the United Kingdom have full air-conditioning: even the National Gallery itself does not have it throughout its premises! Is this appropriate and unremarkable, or a shameful neglect of our national treasures, and should we be using more, not less, energy to preserve them? This paper will therefore concentrate on general principles – for existing buildings and systems as well as new ones – and on temperature and humidity rather than lighting or air quality.

A cautionary tale

Naturally, when designing a new or refurbished museum or gallery, both the client and the design-team wish to do their best. At the early stages, at least, energy-efficiency tends to be fairly low on the priority list, both the client and the design team agreeing that 'no effort must be spared to look after this valuable collection; providing the best and most advanced technology to do it: after all, any extra capital, maintenance and energy costs are trivial in relation to the value of the objects displayed'.

As the project proceeds, life gets more complicated: money runs short and the air-conditioning becomes not quite so full: either in itself or in the coverage of the building. But if the objects then enjoy one non-ideal environment when on display, and another when elsewhere or in storage, have we spent our money on the right things? Is the welter of advanced mechanical technology upon which everything depends an unfortunate necessity or a bad habit?[2]

Once the system is running – and it may take a long time to get it to perform adequately – those trivial costs of energy, maintenance, operation and management often prove surprisingly burdensome and suggestions that a prized object might be sold to pay for them are not well received. Economies are therefore sought, often by pruning bits from the system and maybe even by limiting running hours. Has the best then been the enemy of the good? Would a simpler solution to start with actually have been the more effective in practice?

What sort of buildings are we thinking of?

When discussing museums and galleries, one first tends to think of national institutions such as the National Gallery or the Victoria & Albert Museum. One then remembers smaller municipal facilities, and the constellation of private, public and charitable institutions that have mushroomed over the years. And what about buildings belonging to the National Trust, English Heritage and others? All these fall easily into the Chambers Dictionary definition of a museum as '. . . a repository for the collection, exhibition, and study of objects . . .', and I would like to consider them all here. Most of the underlying environmental require-ments are similar, though the solutions differ; some are transferable, others are not.

Is energy efficiency important?

Over the past half-century, there have been a number of pressing reasons why we should use fuel wisely: in the 1940s it was availability, in the 1950s air pollution, in the 1960s we had a holiday, but in the early 1970s came concern about resource depletion followed rapidly by the oil crisis, political problems, and rising costs. In the early 1980s the Iranian crisis gave a second twist to the knife. In the late 1980s we were back on holiday again, with energy-costs in real terms falling back more-or-less to 1960s levels. Then the air-pollution argument came back, but now on a global scale, and many people are now making pious noises but not necessarily doing very much.

Although the prime reasons have gone in and out of fashion, the underlying requirement seems to be here to stay, and it is becoming a professional – and indeed moral – requirement to avoid unnecessary energy-use, certainly where this can be done (as it often can) at little or no additional cost. The architects' and building services engineers' institutions have already nailed their colours to this mast. However, energy efficiency needs to be seen as just one of many performance criteria that need to be met simultaneously: not as an end in itself, more a reward for a good job well-done. It should not be attained by compromising the prime requirements, though those requirements should be questioned if they seem to get in the way of simple, sensible and effective solutions.
To achieve energy efficiency requires:

  i. clear intentions.
 ii. good design with appropriate technology.
iii. careful execution with attention to detail.
 iv. effective operation and management.

To get the best result, all these criteria need to be met simultaneously: quite a tall order – often good ideas get compromised in the follow-through. The requirements also interact: for example, is poor system performance a consequence of inadequate maintenance and management, or was the design too complicated for the management and maintenance skills and budgets realistically likely to have been available? As usual, the answers often lie somewhere in the middle.

I would like to introduce another concept: avoiding energy-dependency. In principle it seems unwise to create situations where maintaining an acceptable environment relies entirely on high-energy flows and the operation of extensive plant in avoidable situations. Energy-dependency tends to bring with it fragility: if something goes wrong, conditions can change dramatically (Fig. 1). It is rare to find organisations whose air-conditioning systems have not let them down in this way. The situation in Figure 1 occurred typically once or twice a year until the controls were altered to shut the system down when such a situation developed, which always seemed to occur at the weekend or over Christmas! However, in principle, it seems to me safer to seek solutions which come to a natural equilibrium and which use low-capacity systems where necessary to fine-tune improvements.

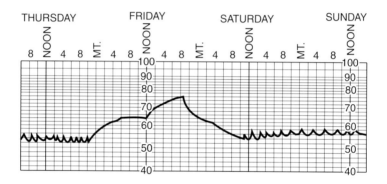

Figure 1 Cyclic fluctuations of 'controlled' relative humidity and consequences of a control failure.

Is it complicated and does it cost a lot?

In the past twenty years, through hard experience and government-sponsored research, demonstration and best practice projects, we have learnt a lot about making buildings more energy efficient. Although few of these projects are directly relevant to museums and galleries – being a relatively small market with very specific individual requirements – the following generalisations seem to be widely applicable:

1. Environmental and performance standards need careful review, but one does not have to lower them, as was assumed in the 'Save It' era. Indeed, they can often be raised.
2. It is not necessary to adopt alternative lifestyles: the best results often come from recognising people's needs, and helping to make the correct behaviour intuitively obvious.
3. Bolt-on technology is seldom the answer. Like many 'go-faster' gadgets, it seldom works as well as intended and tends to fall-off again! The best results come from an integrated approach with the appropriate technology in the right place: often by improving the performance of something you need to have anyway – such as a boiler, a

window, controls or a light-fitting, rather than adding extra things that need to be looked after specially.

4. Designers can only do so much. The management and users have a large influence on the final result, generally the more so the larger and more highly serviced the building. However, there are ways of making their lives easier.

5. High-capital investment is not a pre-requisite. On new projects, items which look expensive are often affordable within the overall project budget. For instance, a structure with better thermal performance may cost more but reduce the costs of, and in places perhaps even the need for, air-conditioning plant. In existing buildings, energy-saving measures which would be expensive in their own right can become more cost-effective, if undertaken as part of normal maintenance and refurbishment cycles.

What should the design criteria be?

The thermal environment in museums and galleries has to satisfy three different sets of requirements:

1. *Preservation and display of the contents:* as a general rule, these are not very sensitive to temperature (though low temperatures tend to slow down chemical and biological decay) and much more sensitive to moisture, for which relative humidity is the normal, but not always an entirely appropriate, proxy. Dryness leads to shrinkage and embrittlement; dampness and poor ventilation to corrosion, mould and insect attack; and moisture fluctuations to dimensional changes (which cause surface damage and loosen surface layers) and sometimes even to condensation.

2. *Human comfort:* normally clothed people prefer a higher temperature than most objects require for optimum preservation, but people are not sensitive to relative humidity within quite a broad range.

3. *The well-being of the building:* like the contents, buildings are reasonably tolerant of changes in temperature and are more affected by moisture, and particularly condensation. These arguments are developed further elsewhere.[5]

Somehow all these conflicting requirements have to be balanced, and a suitable compromise reached between comfort, well-being of exhibits, display of exhibits, preservation of the building, and energy and cost-efficient operation. Traditionally the 'best' compromise has been one of high energy, high-capital cost and high fragility: heating or cooling to obtain comfort temperatures for the people (maintained constantly to avoid disturbing the contents), humidity control to recommended levels of RH, and engineering the building so that it can tolerate the consequences.

Commonly, however, the solutions do not hang together, the balance often becomes lopsided, and the collection and/or the building suffers. For example, the *low temperatures* for optimum preservation are not very comfortable and require cooling, dehumidification and fan-energy inputs in summer. In any event, *comfort usually over-rides conservation*, making the building hotter and drier in winter than is good for at least some objects. If winter humidification is provided for the good of the collection, condensation can occur causing the building to deteriorate. *Dual standards* apply, with full environmental control limited to key display areas only, in which individual objects may be for only a small proportion of their lives. For example, in one gallery which I surveyed, great attempts had been made to protect the display galleries from the hostile external environment by surrounding them with ancillary areas such as – you've guessed it – the storerooms! *Energy-saving overrides conservation*, most commonly when:

i. the hours of plant operation are restricted to hours of occupancy and the collection has to fend for itself at other times.

ii. the start of the heating season is delayed to the last possible moment, allowing the building to become relatively cold and damp. When the heating at last comes on, temperature and humidity conditions fluctuate rapidly, causing stress to the objects. A similar situation may apply if cooling is available but its use is delayed.

iii. Sometimes *silly things* happen too, for instance in one museum the extract air from all three air-handling plants went into a common exhaust plenum from which part was recirculated back into the museum. Unfortunately, one of the air handlers served the restaurant!

The role of recommended standards

So what is the job and how does it vary? Are the solutions appropriate for the whole range of institutions, from a national museum to a local museum or a stately home? Of course not. But too often people jump to the numbers in the standards book without thinking through the real requirements, and then either follow them slavishly or reject them totally if they seem to be unrealistic.

I would like to see standards as a starting point and not the Holy Grail. For example, take BS 5454: Recommendations for Storage and Exhibition of Archival Documents.[3] It points out correctly that unsuitable environments have caused more damage to valuable objects than any other single factor. In the Foreword, it therefore says it aims 'for the highest standards that limiting factors allow'. But are the highest standards always the appropriate standards? Or is this yet another instance of 'the best is the enemy of the good' syndrome, discussed by Ivan Illich[4] many years ago? We might all aspire to owning a Rolls-Royce, get on perfectly well in a Mini (at lower cost and with less environmental impact) and find that a bicycle offers the best compromise between convenience, economy, energy efficiency and environmental impact, particularly if a Ford or a train is also available for the more arduous trips! To be fair, the Foreword to this British Standard goes on to say that it gives recommendations only, and that many questions can be answered only in the context of local conditions. However, standards seldom seem to be applied in this way: like it or not, the suggestion becomes the norm.

The Standard then goes on to recommend accurate and constant control of the internal environment's temperature and relative humidity, appearing to place no particular weight on either although, as we have seen, stable humidities are usually the more important. It says that its objectives may be achieved either by air-conditioning or by a building or compartment with high thermal inertia.

But here there is a logical inconsistency: as alternatives the two approaches are philosophically different (although they can be used effectively in combination):

i. Air-conditioning can, in principle, be set up to provide nominally accurate and constant control (though as we all know achieving this in practice is not quite so easy, and that temperature is more easily controlled than RH, which tends to fluctuate to a greater or lesser degree, as in Figure 1 before and after the runaway).

ii. The high thermal inertia (and, where possible, moisture-sponge) approach essentially rates stability and robustness over constancy and fragility; the environment finds its own level (albeit often with some mechanical assistance) and then flywheels through the seasons with stable but slowly drifting temperature and RH.

To insist on engineering precision with a flywheel-and-sponge approach is, to my mind, missing the point. But, as Michael Young says(2:p.222), in our technocratic society 'evening out natural fluctuations has become an egalitarian enterprise which it is heresy to question'. But this is essentially a modern obsession, and one has to consider how so many historic objects ever survived into the 20th century without the benefit of modern technology. However, where we must have constant conditions, the flywheel and sponge can often make the engineering systems less costly and energy-consuming, and the resulting environment less energy-dependent.

Low-energy approaches to control of the internal environment

In display areas of national institutions there may be no alternative to full air-conditioning: the crowds of people impose wildly fluctuating heat and moisture loads, and conditions may have to be held at some sort of international standard so that objects can be transferred from museum to museum and country to country without major environmental shock. Even here, to improve energy efficiency, conditions are now beginning to be allowed to drift: a practice which originated, I think, in Canada.

Perhaps we can learn some lessons from what happens to sensitive museum objects in transit. Nobody quite trusts air-conditioned lorries and aeroplane holds, 'buffered' cases and containers are often used, well-insulated and sealed, with hygroscopic equilibrium established between the object and its immediate environment. The same principle is used in buffered display cases which are sometimes used to protect valuable items where there is no air-conditioning or where the prevailing conditions are unsuitable for the object concerned.

A low-energy approach starts with the needs of the collection and an understanding of the climate. Some items need practically no environmental control; most need some stability of moisture content (however they often tolerate slow drifts as the weather changes) but are fairly indifferent to temperature; others require tighter control. Gary Thomson[10] suggested two grades of control: Class I (fine – though not in fact very fine, allowing ±5% RH and summertime temperatures up to 24°C) and Class II (coarse), to which one could add a lower RH for metals, and – as advocated by the Museums & Galleries Commission – tagging and special treatment of objects with individual needs, for instance those which have been waterlogged and prefer a very humid environment. And remember that, where the conditions are not too bad, things may be happier to stay in equilibrium with the environment they have got used to, rather than being transplanted into the 'best' environment for a typical object of their kind.

Following these lines, it may be helpful to consider not what are the ideal conditions for an object, but to think more in terms of the amount of environmental instability objects can reasonably endure. If such a risk-management approach seems rather cavalier, remember that the lux-hour approach to conservation lighting already follows similar lines: there is little point in preserving an important object if nobody can see it, but one can limit its deterioration to an acceptably low level!

The relative humidity of the outside air in the UK tends to average around 80% in winter and 70% in summer. Owing to the psychrometrics only the summer air is damp inside a heated building; in winter the air is usually too dry, as Figure 2 shows. Compare this with Figure 3, which indicates the temperature to which a room would have to be heated for the outside air to give an average 50% RH (both examples excluding internal moisture gains, which might add 5% or so). While the example in Figure 2 would require not only powerful wintertime heating but also humidification, Figure 1 requires less heat and no humidification: a much lower-energy strategy. Now maybe people would object to wandering round cold museums, and the attendants in particular to sitting in them (though local heating could be provided), such a free-running approach may well be beneficial in seasonally used facilities and in storage areas. Now this is not heresy: museums are already doing or advocating it, for example, The National Trust with their 'conservation heating' of buildings which are shut in winter.[6,7] Up to a point, this control of heating for constant RH – rather than constant air temperature – may well reproduce what happened in the past, where buildings with coal and wood fires had high ventilation rates, fairly poorly controlled but relatively low-powered heating, and relatively low-air temperatures generally!

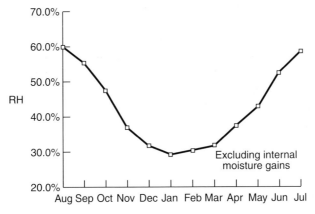

Figure 2 Average monthly internal relative humidity in space maintained at 20°C in London.

Researchers at the National Museum of Denmark (8) have advocated a rather similar approach for museum and archive stores, and indeed some poorly heated stores may sometimes achieve good conditions by default. However, by computer modelling they suggest that where a room contains a large area of hygroscopic material, attempts to lower RH by increasing temperature can cause instability: conditions can be created in which warming up the contents drives off moisture and humidifies the air! Instead, they advocate very low-powered fresh-air ventilation systems with dehumidification where necessary. They consider 'the quick, nervous reaction of orthodox air-conditioning is unnecessary and wasteful when used to control the sluggishly reacting mass of objects in a well-insulated store: a gentle push towards the right moisture content is all that is needed'.

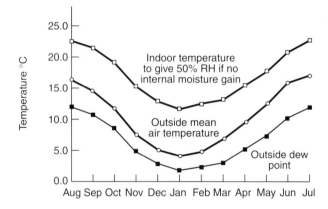

Figure 3 London monthly average outside conditions and required internal air temperature to bring this air to 50% RH.

Determining the priorities

I have talked perhaps too much about standards and about unusual low-energy approaches. But in most buildings – both existing and proposed – work sponsored by the Energy Efficiency Office and others has shown that major economies are usually possible without changing the rules – just by doing the simple things well.

The Building Research Energy Conservation Support Unit (BRECSU) has recently coined a term for it – minimising avoidable waste. And there is a lot of avoidable waste around. For new buildings effective design and planning can be used to reduce the energy requirements and energy-dependency of the building and the loads falling on the building services. The services themselves can be better designed using a number of straightforward rules:

i. Select efficient equipment. This can be particularly rewarding for those objects in museums and galleries which run for twenty-four hours per day. Make sure, too, that these systems are restricted to the areas which really need them!

ii. Consider part-load operation. Often systems are designed to meet the worst case and run uneconomically at other times. For example, heating plant sized to meet peak wintertime loads may operate uneconomically for most of the year, particularly if it stays on in summer for border-line duties. Fortunately well-controlled modern condensing gas boilers can solve a lot of these problems, but to date very few people have been specifying them.

iii. Avoid the 'tail wags the dog effect' where large systems have to remain on to service very localised needs in space or time. Try to provide for these individually.

iv. Understand where the energy is going. The instant reaction is that energy efficiency is predominantly about heating and insulation, but electricity tends to cost four or five times as much per delivered unit and generates 2.5 to 3.4 times as much carbon dioxide as oil or gas respectively. In air-conditioning systems, fans and humidity control systems tend to be the hidden energy-wasters. Consider their design and operation carefully: is heat fighting cool for humidity control and should the fans really have to run flat out all night?

v. Avoid unnecessary technology. It is usually best to do what you have to as well as possible before starting to superimpose systems to try and do it better.

vi. Provide effective and user-friendly control and monitoring systems with suitable reporting and alarm facilities. And try to make sure that it switches plant right off when it is not needed: all too often things stay on unnecessarily 'just in case', for situations which it should be possible to anticipate.

vii. Consider the ordinary systems too: domestic hot water, the offices, the restaurant, lighting and ventilation in the corridors and toilets – often they give rich pickings.

viii. Make sure that the appropriate person or persons 'owns' the task of running the building both well and energy-efficiently.

Conclusion

I can do no better than to quote Gary Thomson[9] who used to be Scientific Adviser at the National Gallery: 'There is something inelegant in the mass of energy-consuming machinery needed at present to maintain constant RH and illuminance, something inappropriate in an expense which is beyond most of the world's museums. Thus the trend must be towards simplicity, reliability and cheapness. We cannot, of course, prophesy what will be developed, but I should guess that it will include means for stabilising the RH in showcases without machinery, use of solar energy for RH control in the tropics, improved building construction to reduce energy losses, and extensive electronic monitoring'. Fifteen years later the prospects sound rather similar, but we now have more of the tools and more of the reasons to use them. Let's get on with it!

References

1. de Guichen, G., 'Preventive Conservation in Museums', ICCROM/PSD seminar, Victoria & Albert Museum, April 1984.

2. Young, M., *The Metronomic Society*, Thames & Hudson, 1988.

3. British Standards Institution, BS Recommendations for Storage and Exhibition of Archival Documents, BS 5454:1989.

4. Illich, I., *Energy and Equity*, Calder & Boyars, 1974.

5. Bordass, W. T., 'The Effects – For Good and Ill – Of Building Services and Their Controls' in Proceedings of the First International Conference on Building Pathology, Oxford, 25–27 September 1989 (Hutton+Rostron, Gomshall, Surrey GU5 9QA, 1989).

6. Staniforth S. and Hayes B., 'Keep the Old Piles Standing', *New Scientist*, 1989, pp. 37–41.

7. Staniforth S. and Hayes B., 'Evidence of Environmental Problems in Historic Houses and the Illustration of Some Practical Solutions' in Proceedings of the Second International Conference on Building Pathology, Cambridge, 24–26 September 1990, (Hutton+Rostron, Gomshall, Surrey GU5 9QA, 1990).

8. Padfield T. and Jensen P., *Low Energy Climate Control in Museum Stores*, Conservation Department, National Museum of Denmark, Lyngby, 1990.

9. Thomson G., *The Museum Environment*, First edition, Butterworths, 1978.

10. Thomson G., 'Draft Specification for the Museum Exhibition Environment', ICCROM/PSD seminar, Victoria & Albert Museum, April 1984.

Biography

William Bordass is a scientist who has had a long practical interest in the design and performance of buildings. Following research in physical chemistry at Cambridge, he held many responsibilities within the architectural and engineering practice of Robert Matthew, Johnson-Marshall & Partners (now RMJM Ltd), where in 1975 he was made Associate responsible for developing the building services engineering group and later a specialist team which concentrated on investigations of environmental and energy performance. In 1983 he set up William Bordass Associates which works largely on design briefs, on field and desk studies of building performance and building research management, with particular reference to environmental control, energy efficiency, new technology and physical and chemical deterioration in existing, proposed and historic buildings. He has carried out a number of energy and environmental surveys on museums and historic buildings.

He was founder chairman of the multiprofessional London Energy Group and has worked on a range of projects for the Department of Energy and the Building Research Establishment.

A Survey of Energy Use in Museums and Galleries

Tadj Oreszczyn PhD MInstE CEng MCIBSE, **Tim Mullany** BA(Econ) BA(Arch) and **Caitriona Ni Riain** The Bartlett Graduate School, University College London

Why save energy?

The world's limited fossil fuel resource has been one of the chief motivating forces for saving energy over the past twenty years. In particular, reserves of oil would be depleted by the year 2035 if current energy consumption continues unabated. Furthermore, over 50% of the remaining reserves are located in one very small geographical area, the Middle East.

Global warming

However, over the last couple of years, the argument for reducing the burning of fossil fuels has shifted towards reducing emissions of carbon dioxide, which are thought to be one of the main causes of global warming. The burning of all fossil fuels results in the emission of carbon dioxide. At the current rate of emission, it is predicted that the earth's temperature will rise resulting in catastrophic changes to the world's climate. Consequently, the UK government has set a minimum target of stabilising emissions of carbon dioxide at 1990 levels by the year 2005. If nothing is done to reduce energy consumption, government projections suggest a growth in emissions of between 10 and 40% over the next 15 years. Reducing energy-use in buildings is seen as one of the most practical and cost-effective means of achieving this target.

Current fuel prices do not represent the true environmental cost of global warming. Various schemes are at present under debate both by the Department of Environment and the EC to change this situation. For example, the EC had been considering adopting a carbon tax of $3 a barrel in 1993 which would have increased to $10 a barrel by the year 2000.[1] This would increase the real price of fossil fuels by 50% by the year 2000. So, over the coming decade energy issues are likely to increase in importance.

Energy efficiency not just energy saving

The easiest way to save energy is simply to switch off our energy-intensive appliances. The aims of energy efficiency, however, are different. Energy efficiency aims to reduce energy consumption without reducing standards, be they standards of thermal comfort for people or, in the case of museums, environmental requirements of objects. Organisations such as the Energy Efficiency Office (EEO) are trying to encourage energy saving while at the same time maintaining or improving standards.

For museums the chief motivation for energy efficiency is one of reducing operating costs. Museums are being encouraged to manage their resources more efficiently – this includes the use of energy. As fuel resources near depletion, fuel costs rise, and, as a consequence, there is increased pressure to reduce energy consumption. The current cost of fossil fuels represents the value that is put on remaining fossil fuels plus their production costs.

Museums should however note that if a policy of energy efficiency is not adopted and global warming escalates, or fossil fuels become scarcer, there may come a time when the pressure to save energy will become so great that the opportunity to undertake measures to maintain or improve standards is lost. Clearly it is in the interest of museums to act now to save energy in a way which improves standards of object care.

The aims of this paper are to quantify current energy-use in museums and determine what, if any, impedances to energy efficiency exist. The method adopted was to survey current energy-use and attitudes of museums to energy efficiency by sending a questionnaire to 100 museums followed by a visit to 6 of these museums which had largely differing energy consumptions. The results from this questionnaire and visits form the main part of this paper.

Questionnaire

Energy data collection was carried out in the summer of 1991 by means of a questionnaire in two parts which was sent to a sample of 100 museums (see Appendix A).

Part A of the questionnaire was to be completed by the museum's director/senior administrator and was designed specifically to identify main collection types, hours of opening and energy costs as a percentage of total running costs, both actual and perceived. The aim was also to assess the attitude towards energy-saving measures/ professional advice and the major obstacles to their implementation; whether energy consumption is monitored and/or targeted, and, if so, whether it is the specific responsibility of any one person.

18

Part B was to be completed by 'the person most responsible for energy use in the museum' and was designed to identify total energy consumption, percentages attributable to particular uses and fuel types. Further areas of interest were building considerations such as the nature of the site, the age of the building, the type of construction, the type and age of heating systems and their controls and the nature of lighting and ventilation systems, with particular reference to air-conditioning.

The questionnaire was developed in order to give sufficient data with which to calculate the Normalised Performance Indicator (NPI) as recommended by the EEO. This should allow comparison of energy efficiency for museums of various sizes, opening hours and climate.

By means of the questionnaire, an understanding could be obtained on how the perception of energy efficiency, both in its overall importance as a percentage of total operating costs and in the effectiveness of energy-saving measures, match up to reality as indicated by the collected data. It also served to identify the obstacles to implementing energy-efficient measures, as perceived by museum directors. The usefulness of the NPI was evaluated and found to be lacking as an indicator of fuel cost and environmental impact.

Finally, the intention was also to draw conclusions from the data concerning types of fuel used and the means by which it is used, the relationship between lighting and heating and the effects on energy efficiency of partial or full air-conditioning, building type and the age/efficiency of the main heating boiler.

Sample

A sample of 100 museums representative in terms of energy-use of the wide range of museums in the UK, had to be selected. Unfortunately, there is little available data by which to check just how representative the sample is. The sample was selected on the basis of the following criteria:

   i. The main collection type.
   ii. The floor area of the museum/gallery building.

Museums were selected in proportion to the total number of museums in each particular category of main collection type, and, as far as possible, the floor area of the building.

The main sources for this information were *The Museums Yearbook*[2] and *Museums and Galleries* 1991.[3] The possibility of using the Museums & Galleries Commission Registration Database was investigated but details of collection types are not yet available on the database.

Response rates

A 43% response to the questionnaire was received despite numerous efforts to extract responses from the remaining 57%. Typical reasons given for no responses were: 'this is the worst time of year as the person who would deal with it is on holiday'; 'we are short staffed'; 'the question-naire is asking questions we cannot answer'; 'bills are dealt with centrally' and 'we share services with other buildings'.

All of these are perfectly plausible reasons although it does indicate that the museums who responded may be ones which are more aware of, and concerned with, energy-related issues.

The undertaking that those who responded in full would be provided with results of their own individual energy calculation and how this compared with other museums was clearly insufficient inducement. It begs the question as to why the inducement was not attractive enough if genuine concern exits about energy performance, both in real and relative terms, and if not, why importance was not attached to energy efficiency and performance. A reasonable conclusion may be that those museums that did not respond are precisely those which would benefit from a greater understanding of the problems.

Reliability

The results arising out of the questionnaire and the conclusions that have been drawn, rely entirely on the quality of the responses. Major obvious discrepancies were double-checked and were found to result directly from incorrect data. Undoubtedly other perhaps less obvious mistakes are present in the data. Other similar exercises carried out in the examination of office buildings have encountered similar problems of data reliability.

Questionnaire findings
Fuel costs as a proportion of running costs (perception vs reality)

Notwithstanding the areas of difficulty in obtaining detailed figures for energy consumption, expressed by individual museums, interesting comparisons can be made between 'actual' and 'best guess' in relation to what percentage of total operating (variable) costs of which energy accounts.

The inability to obtain the information regarding actual energy costs gives us the opportunity to compare 'actual' and 'best guess' or the perceived importance of energy. Encouragingly, slightly over half those who responded actually knew what percentage of their total operating costs went on energy. The average was 6 per cent but the range varied from

2% to 25%. This average figure compares reasonably well with other building types.

Interestingly and surprisingly, however, the museums that guessed the percentage of total operating costs (in excess of 50% of the sample) perceived on average that energy accounted for 12% of the total operating costs, i.e. twice the value of the average 'actual' figure. Also, only 10% perceived their energy performance to be good. This is interesting for a number of reasons. It indicates that the perception by management of energy-use may be greater than it is in reality. This perception may well have an effect on attitudes to energy-saving measures and their ultimate effectiveness. Over 50% had implemented one energy-saving measure during the last five years, although half of the measures were modifications to light fittings, followed by changes to controls and the fitting of draught stripping. Only 5 had carried out more than one measure and only 2 had been able to address a wide range of issues such as installing insulation and good housekeeping.

Clearly, given the apparent awareness of the problem, there must be major constraints which are preventing reasonable cost-effective energy-conservation measures from being undertaken. The most significant factor which was perceived as an obstacle was lack of capital. This seems unfortunate as many energy-conservation measures have a pay-back period of less than 4 years. Also, there are often energy-efficient measures which require little capital such as good housekeeping. The physical constraints imposed by the building itself were seen as the next most significant obstacle. These constraints are clearly important for measures such as improving insulation of walls, windows and floors. They are less of a barrier when considering replacement of a boiler, for example. Interestingly, the third factor which was seen to limit energy-saving measures was that of environmental control. The view was given that the saving of energy would reduce the degree of environmental control required for objects thus making such measures unacceptable on museum conservation grounds.

These museums did not understand that energy efficiency aims to minimise the use of energy whilst maintaining, or improving, standards and which, in the case of museums, environmental control is of paramount importance.

Around 70% of museums thought that their environment was adequate in full or in part for visitors, whilst more than 60% felt that the environment was not adequate for the exhibits. It is encouraging that since the main reason given for this perceived inadequacy is lack of control over temperature, there is considerable scope for improvements in energy-saving together while promoting environment stability.

Professional advice

It is encouraging that approximately half of the museums that responded had sought some professional advice. This was mostly from specialist consultants or heating and ventilating engineers. Four museums obtained advice from the Fuel Boards and one from an Area Museum Council.

Monitoring and targeting

Half the museums reported that they monitored regularly their fuel bills although only six actually set a target. This was often a financial target of not spending more than the previous year, rather than an energy-conservation target. It did not appear that any museum set rolling-energy targets, based, for example, on degree-day behaviour, to get advance warning of high energy consumption.

Energy responsibility

The person who was responsible for day-to-day energy management varied. In smaller museums it is the curator, in medium-sized museums it is estate managers and building services engineers and energy-conservation officers in larger museums.

To summarise, clearly much has been achieved over the last five years in terms of energy awareness. It appears that a large number of institutions actually know how much energy they are using. Those that do not know actually perceive the problem to be more severe than it is in reality. Also, people are prepared to take some action where the measures are easy to achieve and the pay-back small. However, many museums are not undertaking more because they feel that improvements are expensive and difficult to carry out, or that they are detrimental to the environment of the collection.

Normalised performance indicator

In order to compare the energy consumption of different museums, the Normalised Performance Indicator (NPI) is often used. The NPI compares the energy performance of different buildings taking into account several different factors that contribute to additional energy usage, i.e. floor area, local climate and hours of use. In this way, museums of different size, or location can be compared on the same basis. The NPI can therefore be seen as an energy label for buildings, similar say to the miles per gallon rating used to compare the energy performance of cars.

The NPI is currently the main method of comparing energy efficiency generally for the entire building stock. It also appears in Energy Efficiency for Libraries, Museums, Art Galleries, and Churches published in 1989 by the EEO.[4] It is also the main method of analysis for energy-use in museums recommended in the Audit Commission's report on Local Authorities published in 1990. However, the NPI was not developed specifically for museums.

An NPI of less than 220 is considered a good energy-efficiency rating by the EEO, between 220 and 310 fair, and more than 310 poor. Just over 50% of the museums rated poor on this scale.

Figure 1 shows the calculated NPI for the 28 museums who provided adequate data to perform this analysis. These are listed in increasing NPI from left to right on the figure. Not all museums could provide sufficient data to calculate the NPI. One reason is that not all museums' energy-use is metered separately.

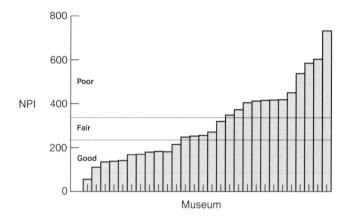

Figure 1 Museums listed in ascending order of Normalised Performance Indicator.

The questionnaire asked museums to rate the energy efficiency of their museum and this is displayed in Figure 2 on the graph of NPI. Only one museum rated its performance as good. Clearly many seemed to be over-pessimistic. It is therefore unlikely that calculating the NPI will stir people into taking more action than they have already. In fact, several energy professionals now think that the NPI is not a satisfactory way of comparing energy-use in buildings. This is mainly because it is not a good comparator of fuel costs, which is what interests most building managers. Figure 3 shows not only the NPI, but also the fuel cost per square metre for each museum. Some museums have a similar NPI to others but an energy bill which is twice as large. This is because these museums use a greater amount of electricity. Also, the NPI hides the true consumption of energy. To calculate the NPI, the energy as delivered to the doorstep of the building is used. This neglects the fact that energy is also used to bring energy to the doorstep and that this energy must also be paid for. This is particularly important in the case of electricity which requires four units of fossil fuel energy to produce one unit of electrical energy. For this reason on-peak electricity is approximately four times more expensive for the consumer than, say, gas, per unit of delivered energy.

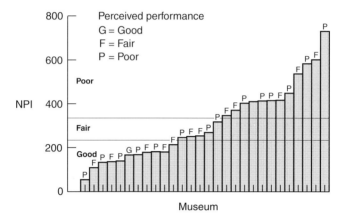

Figure 2 Museums perceived energy performance and Normalised Performance Indicator.

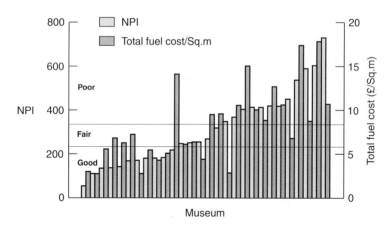

Figure 3 Annual fuel cost per square metre and Normalised Performance Indicator listed in ascending order of NPI.

The NPI is particularly not well-suited for use in museum buildings because of the diverse nature of museum buildings and their operation. Comparing museums with different NPI means that very rarely is like with like being compared. For example, the NPI calculation should strictly only be used for museums open between 1,900 and 3,790 hours a year. Unfortunately nine out of the 28 museums responding to the question-naire, i.e. one-third, have opening hours greater or smaller than this. For these museums the NPI rating is not strictly applicable. Also which hours should a museum use to calculate its NPI? The hours of public use, the hours of worker use or the hours of object use? Most museums are now controlling the environment for conservation reasons, i.e. the objects as well as visitors, so the hours of object-use, i.e. twenty-four hours per day, should perhaps be taken. Because of these problems with the NPI, the absolute annual fuel cost divided by the total floor area of the museums has also been used to compare energy-use in different museums.

Fuel cost

Figure 4 shows the annual fuel cost divided by the total floor area. This ranges from 94p/m² to £21.38/m². The average is £7/m². This compares with approximately £10 found in a similar study of office buildings.

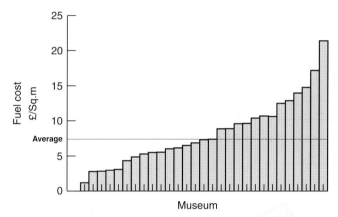

Figure 4   Museums listed in ascending order of annual fuel cost per square metre.

The average energy cost for museums was £68,000 per annum, although this varied from as little as £540 a year to half a million pounds. If our sample is representative of museums in the UK, and there are 2,000 museums in the UK, then the total energy bill for the UK would be £140 million a year. This is more than likely an overestimation as a greater response from the larger museums is likely to have been received. This would mean that museums account for less than 1% of the UK energy-use in buildings. For this reason, it is unlikely that museums will receive any preferential treatment or particular attention at a national level.

Figure 5 shows the same data as Figure 4, but now the bar for each museum has been marked according to the museum's perception of the performance of the building – good, fair or poor. Clearly there is no feel for telling how good or bad energy-performers museum buildings are. This phenomenon is not specific to museums. A recent survey[5] examined energy-use in offices considered to be exemplars of energy-efficient design. Inspection of their fuel bills however showed that they performed no better than some buildings which had been designed without any special consideration for energy efficiency.

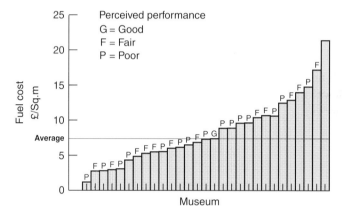

Figure 5 Museums perceived energy performance listed in ascending order of annual fuel cost per square metre.

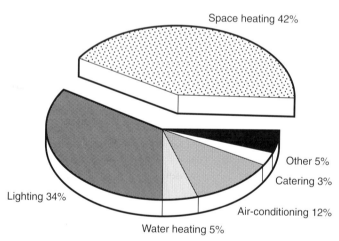

Figure 6 Fuel cost by use as perceived by museum respondents.

Energy use

Figure 6 shows a breakdown of the fuel cost by energy-use as perceived by the respondents. The greatest perceived use of energy is to provide space heating and lighting which together accounts for a total of 76%. Lighting on its own consumes just over one third of the cost. This fact is often hidden, if energy not cost is calculated, because electricity is expensive.

Figure 7 shows the proportion of the total cost that is space heating. On average, space heating accounted for 42% of the cost but this varied from 9% to 90%. So space heating can be quite an insignificant proportion of energy consumption for some buildings. Since, however, space heating can account for a large proportion of energy costs it is interesting to compare the use that is made of museum space (Fig. 8). Just over 50% is used for displaying objects, 13% for storage and the rest for general circulation, offices, etc. Surprisingly, almost 20% of the space is used for general circulation. Often forgotten is that, on average, one-third of the space is not used for storage or exhibition. Note that these results agree closely with those obtained by Lord & Nicks[6] during their study on the cost of collecting.

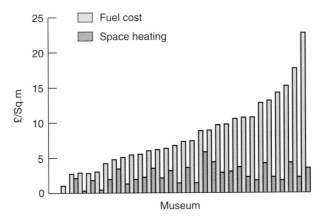

Figure 7 Total fuel cost and space heating cost per square metre.

Parameters affecting energy consumption

In order to determine the main factors which affect energy consumption in museums, the age and size of the building and whether it is air-conditioned, the main type of collection and whether the museum is a national or non-national museum have been investigated.

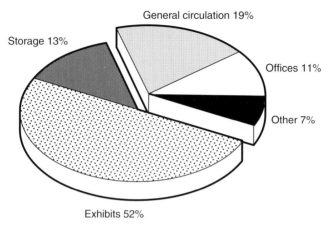

Figure 8 Use of floor space in museums.

Museum age

Figure 9 shows both the age and fuel cost for each museum. Only two of the 43 museums that responded were built since building regulations began to include control of the thermal performance of buildings. Therefore one would perhaps not expect age to play a significant part. Perhaps surprisingly, the older buildings appear to be the most energy-efficient.

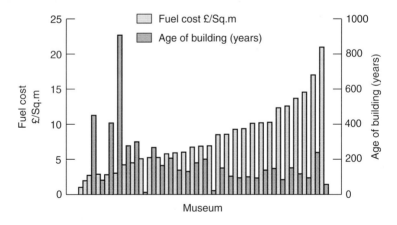

Figure 9 Age of museum listed in ascending order of annual fuel cost per square metre.

Collection type

Figure 10 shows the main type of collection at each museum. There appears to be no very clear relationship between energy consumption and type of collection. However, mixed and fine-art collections are above-average energy consumers.

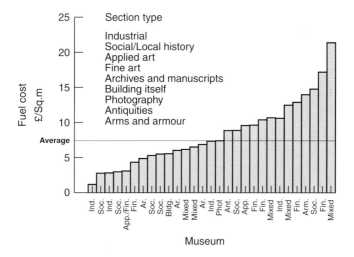

Figure 10   Collection type listed in ascending order of annual fuel cost per square metre.

Museum size

Figure 11 shows the variation in total floor area and fuel cost. There appears to be no clear correlation between fuel cost per square metre and total floor area.

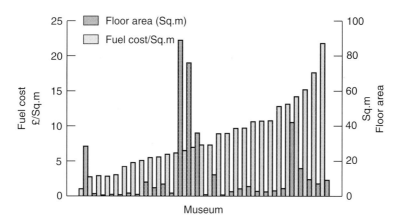

Figure 11   Total floor area listed in ascending order of annual fuel cost per square metre.

Opening hours

Figure 12 shows the annual museum opening hours. There is clearly very little correlation between energy-use and opening hours, except for, perhaps, the very low-energy consumers.

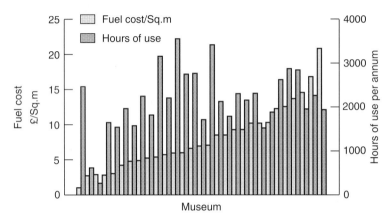

Figure 12 Hours of museum use per hour in ascending order of annual fuel cost per square metre.

National galleries

Figure 13 highlights the national museums. These appear to use either average or slightly more than average energy. The high-energy users are those which are fully air-conditioned.

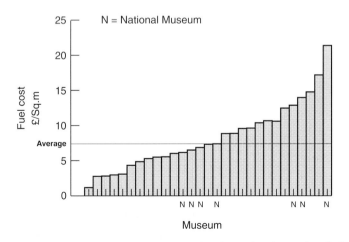

Figure 13 National and non-national museums listed in order of ascending fuel cost.

Air-conditioning

Figure 14 shows the fuel costs for museums with no air-conditioning, those with only part of the building air-conditioned, and those with no ducted air-conditioning but which may have local humidification or dehumidification. On average, non air-conditioned buildings cost less than the partially and full air-conditioned ones, as might be expected. The more interesting finding is that the worst non air-conditioned building uses twice the energy of the best air-conditioned building.

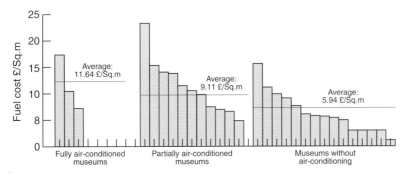

Figure 14   Annual fuel cost per square metre for museums with full, partial and no air-conditioning.

In all types of building there are some which use twice the energy-used by others. A similar finding has been reported in offices (Fig. 15).

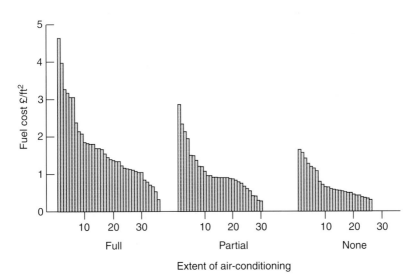

Figure 15   Total energy costs and extent of air conditioning in offices. Source: Energy Consumption Guide 10, Best Practice Programme, BRECSU, May 1991.

Energy efficiency and its potential in museums

It is very easy to adopt a negative attitude to energy efficiency in museums. Museums are often housed in difficult buildings; strict environmental control is demanded; they often have very large spaces. Buildings are often old and listed with old services. However the above shows that there is a wide range of energy consumption among museums and so considerable potential for improvement among different museums exists. Some of the available options revealed by the survey are discussed below.

Space heating
Demand temperature

Figure 16 shows the thermostat temperature settings in the galleries of museums that responded to the questionnaire. Some 40% of the buildings had gallery thermostats set to higher than the legal **maximum** of 19°C. Legislation has been in force since the 1970s to control the maximum temperature in public buildings. In 1980 the maximum heated temperature of public buildings was set to 19°C by the Fuel and Electricity (Heating) (Control) (Amendment) Order.[7] Note, the Factories Act,[8] 1961 and the Offices, Shops and Railways Premises Act, 1963,[9] specify minimum temperatures of 15.5°C and 16°C respectively to be reached within one hour of occupation. Museums are not unique in breaking the maximum legal temperature of 19°C, as similar surveys in other buildings have revealed the same practice. Nobody has been prosecuted under this legislation but neither has this law been repealed. There is some pressure on the government to enforce this legislation. Assuming an average external temperature of 6°C, each 1°C drop will save approximately 8% of the space heating bill. Enforcing this law could be seen as introducing energy-saving legislation and not energy-efficiency legislation. If people like to heat to higher temperatures, why should they not do so?

In museums there can be good reasons for reducing the demand temperature other than just to save energy. The lower the temperature the slower the rate of decay of most museum materials. Temperatures as high as 21°C are good comfort temperatures for lightly clothed sedentary office workers, but is it appropriate for museum visitors who are not sedentary? Clearly museum gallery staff who may be sedentary need to be catered for by, for example, extra clothing.

32

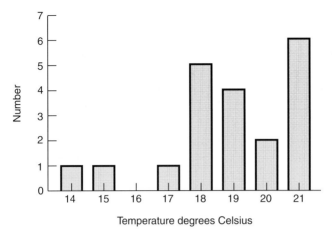

Figure 16 Space heating thermostat settings in the galleries of museums that responded to the questionnaire.

Maintaining a stable relative humidity in museums is considered more important for conservation reasons than a stable temperature. During the heating season the main problem is one of low relative humidity, the higher the air temperature maintained in the building, the more humidification is required. Maintaining lower temperatures during the heating season should therefore reduce the demand for humidification in most museums. For reasons of health, steam humidification is being increasingly used, but this also increases the energy consumption. Reducing the temperature may therefore also help to reduce the energy demand for humidification.

Boiler efficiency

There have been considerable advances in boiler efficiency over the last ten years. Modern boilers can achieve efficiencies of 90% compared with old boilers whose efficiencies can be below 60%. Considerable cost savings can and have been made by replacing old boilers. Replacing the boiler can involve considerable expense but this can be recouped in less than two years.[4] Figure 17 shows the number and age of boilers reported in the survey. Seventy-two per cent of them were found to be over ten years old and one of the boilers was sixty-four years old. Clearly for museums which have little capital, knowing that the measure may pay for itself in a couple of years is of little consolation. This is obviously an area where some type of grant scheme may be of great benefit. Almost 20% of sites had a shared boiler and this makes monitoring improvements and changing a boiler very difficult.

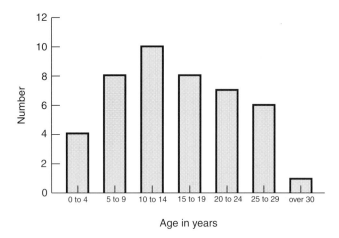

Figure 17 Number and age of space heating boilers in museums and galleries.

The main fuel for space-heating was gas (60% of users). This was then followed equally by electric, oil and coal. Changing fuel for heating from using electricity to gas can be very efficient, depending on the tariff system for heating. The main fuel for water heating was electricity.

Fabric

As pointed out earlier, the majority of buildings were built before any regulatory requirements for energy conservation. As a consequence, insulation in the walls is rare. Most buildings had solid masonry walls, pitched slate roofs and single glazed windows. However, the older buildings appeared to be more energy efficient (see *Museum age* above).

Lighting

This is the second largest energy cost. Encouragingly over half the institutions had fitted low-energy light bulbs. This message seems at longlast to have got through. However less than one-quarter had any automatic lighting control and only 40% of the respondents cleaned light-fittings more than once a year. Cleaning fittings improves the efficiency of light output.

Of all the measures museums had taken, low-energy lighting installations had been high. The lighting of storage areas often only used by a few people can be considerably reduced at great environmental advantage to the collection. Lighting is the case where 'switch off' means energy efficiency, energy-saving and also protection for the collection.

Conclusions

Encouragingly, approximately half of the museums who had responded to the questionnaire had sought some professional energy advice, but it was mainly with organisations with whom the museum had regular contact regarding the building services, and very rarely energy specialists. Currently the Energy Efficiency Office is arranging grants to assist with such advice. The only source of written advice specifically for museums is the EEO booklet mentioned earlier. Most museums were not aware of this prior to contact being made about the survey. The EEO booklet on museums is one in a series of many different building types and does not take into account the specific requirements of environmental control in museums. In order to compare the energy performance of different museums this document uses the Normalised Performance Indicator. This rating is found to be inappropriate, particularly for museums, for the following reasons:

1. The comparison is based on delivered energy which is not a good indicator of either the energy cost or the environmental pollution associated with energy-use. This is principally because one unit of delivered electricity costs four times more than other sources of energy such as gas or oil. Thus, buildings which use a lot of on-peak electricity can appear to have a good rating and yet cost a lot to run.
2. The rating is normalised for opening hours; in museums the space is conditioned not for the visitors but the objects. Therefore, the energy consumption for conditioning should not vary with opening time.
3. Normalisation for external temperature is carried out but only for heating. In air-conditioned buildings, however, normalisation should also take into account summer cooling.
4. There is a great potential in making mistakes during calculation. Because the normalisation process involves calculating several dimensional indices, the potential for making mistakes is high.

Adopting a strategic approach

Museums should try to adopt a strategy for attempting to reduce energy consumption, while at the same time improving the environmental performance of the museum. This strategy should examine the following:

1. A clearly identified person whose responsibility is energy efficiency. This person should report to the director. If the person at the top does not treat energy efficiency seriously then neither will anybody else.

2. Policy on energy efficiency. Although fuel bills only form a small part of the running cost of a museum, substantial savings can be achieved while improving environmental control. Many of the measures however require a capital investment. The museum requires to adopt a mechanism for funding such investments. One such mechanism is to use a proportion of energy savings to be invested in future energy efficiency measures.

3. Energy efficiency should always be investigated as part of environmental assessment and conservation, because the two are closely interlinked. Both can benefit from this exercise, and by integrating the two functions from the start, problems can be avoided. Somebody deciding to turn the heating off to save energy may adversely affect the environmental control. In this way it becomes clear that the objective of energy efficiency is to maintain comfortable standards, be that for the visitors, building or objects, while using the minimum amount of energy. Any degradation in these environmental requirements is not energy efficiency.

4. Make maximum use of all available information so that the most informed decisions can be taken. Monitor fuel bills, find out how much energy goes for different uses. Make use of monitored data for conservation. Monitor the extent to which energy-efficiency measures really are behaving the way that you would expect. If your heating is on are your galleries also overheating? If so something is going wrong. Many energy-efficient measures are heavily user dependent. This applies particularly to controls which can result in substantial energy savings but only if used properly.

5. Shop around and make sure you are getting energy at the cheapest cost. A word of warning, however, as today's cheapest energy may not be tomorrow's. Privatisation of the fuel boards is resulting in new tariff systems and a CO_2 tax may become a reality in the very near future which would shift the relative cost of fuels.

6. Tackle the simplest things first. All too often people think that energy efficiency means the addition of insulation. Over 50% of the questionnaire respondents thought that restrictions of the building were a substantial barrier to energy efficiency, but although it is a barrier to some energy efficiency, it is by no means a barrier to all things. The simple installation of a pump for the heating system, the close observation of how the system is used, and perhaps the fitting of a thermostat or humidistat to control the heating for people and the collection, are all simple measures which should be considered before insulation.

References

1. Ministers set off on long haul towards a carbon tax, in *ENDS* Report 201, October 1991, p.32.
2. *The Museums Yearbook*, published annually by the Museums Association.
3. *Museums and Galleries*, 1991, British Leisure Publications.
4. Energy Efficiency Office, *Introduction to Energy Efficiency in Museums, Galleries, Libraries and Churches*, 1994.
5. Energy Efficiency Office, *Energy Efficiency in Office*, Best Practice Programme Energy Consumption Guide No.10, May 1991.
6. Lord, B., Dexter Lord, G. & Nicks J., *The Cost of Collecting Collection Management in UK Museums*, HMSO, 1989, p.28.
7. *Fuel and Electricity (Heating) (Control) (Amendment) Order 1980*, SI 1013, London, HMSO, 1984.
8. *Factories Act 1961*, London, HMSO.
9. *Offices, Shops and Railway Premises Act 1963*, London, HMSO.

Biographies

Tadj Oreszczyn is currently the Director of the Energy Design Advice Scheme, South East Regional Office and Senior Lecturer in Environmental Design and Engineering at the Bartlett Graduate School, Univerisity College London. His main teaching commitment is in the area of energy and health in buildings. While at the Bartlett he has been actively involved in research and consultancy involving environmental monitoring and control of two London art galleries. Before joining the Bartlett he was Senior Energy Consultant for The Energy Conscious Design Partnership (ECD). While at ECD he assisted architects in the design of energy-efficient buildings and worked on the development of a Domestic Energy Label for the Energy Efficiency Office.

Tim Mullany is currently a Research Assistant in the Environmental Design and Engineering Department at the Bartlett. His main work is a three-year PhD research project commissioned by The National Trust to quantify the adverse effects of large numbers of visitors on historic buildings. With the use of structural monitoring techniques he is assessing the effects of heavy dynamic loadings on up to twenty historic buildings with a variety of structural elements and problems. Prior to joining the Bartlett he was Director of R.W. Head Ltd, Building and Restoration Contractors, Brighton, and subsequently, Associate of Andrew Harris Associates, Chartered Architects, London. He has also lectured in applied and building economics at Manchester Polytechnic.

Caitriona Ni Riain assisted the Bartlett with preparing museum surveys between 1990–91 while studying for a physics degree at King's College.

Air-Conditioning, Energy Efficiency and Environmental Control:
Can All Three Co-exist?

Alfred Reading CEng, MIEE, MIMechE, psc

Air-conditioning, energy efficiency and environmental control: can all three co-exist? The answer is 'Yes, to a degree and with difficulty'. In this paper the approach to this answer will be explored and limitations exposed. The starting point must be a definition of the need. In museums and galleries the objective is to show the collection to the visitors in the best possible setting so that their visit, whether for education, research or pleasure is a satisfying experience. It follows that the exhibits should remain in good condition and on display for the longest possible time. All artifacts deteriorate so steps must be taken to prolong their life. How simple or elaborate these steps may be depends so often on the availability of funds, and solutions must be tailored to suit.

The external environment poses threats from dirt, pollution, heat, cold, moisture and light, while threats from the internal environment are mainly due to people. They bring in dirt and generate heat and moisture while they expect warmth and light. Against all of these dangers most exhibits need protection. The first line of defence is the building itself which ameliorates external conditions. As many of our museums and galleries, and especially stately homes, were built before the scientific understanding of environmental dangers were sufficiently well developed, they are often not ideally suited to this task. Often, exhibits are housed in buildings originally constructed for totally different purposes, so the first step must be to see what can be done to the building to improve its protective function.

Before any action is taken, the specification of the environment to be attained has to be considered carefully. The National Gallery sets an extremely high standard based on the work of a former Scientific Adviser to the Gallery, Garry Thomson, and which is set out in his book, *The Museum Environment*. The control of humidity is paramount and the specified value is normally set at 54%RH ±4%. Temperature is also important. Low stable temperatures, such as the temperature range of 15–16°C as found in the Welsh slate mines in which the National Gallery pictures were stored during the War, are better than those currently specified which have to take into account human-comfort needs. Temperature is held to ±1°C with the mean changing slowly over the range of 19–22°C with the seasons to minimise energy use. For both relative humidity and temperature, within the allowable range the rate of change also matters. Particulate filters to Eurovent 4/5 and carbon filters in accordance with the PSA Report TR70 are used to ensure the removal of dirt and gaseous pollution. Achievement of these standards is expensive both in money and energy. Artifacts other than paintings may have different humidity requirements. The Victoria & Albert Museum requested a 50%RH level with the same tolerance as the best compromise for the varied needs of a mixed collection. For many museums these standards are an impossible dream so the approach must be an attainable stable target which can be maintained.

It is better to have less than ideal conditions which are stable than to have ideal conditions for part of the time and wide fluctuations at other times. This means that turning off the heating at night is an economy which cannot be considered. There may be some merit in reducing ambient temperature at night when lower outside temperatures cause a drop in the internal humidity. This paper describes the steps required to achieve very tight conditions. How far along this path an individual project should be taken will be controlled by the state of the building and available funds.

The building

All buildings leak. This does not refer to rain coming through the roof, though even such gross defects are all too common. Air leakage is less noticeable but has a significant role to play both in energy costs and in its effect on exhibits. Simple theory says 'keep dirty air out' but building occupants require clean air for health reasons, so compromise is necessary. Sealing all the gaps around windows, skylights and any other openings is a start. Some means must be found to have two normally closed doors forming an air lock between the exhibits and the outside so that the benefit of sealing gaps will not be lost. If all this is done successfully, then the building will soon become uncomfortably stuffy. The next stage is to ensure that sufficient filtered fresh air is supplied to the occupants. The CIBSE Guide recommends a generous 8 litres per second per person. Various systems for regulating fresh air supply by sensing carbon dioxide in the space are available, and implementing them would dramatically reduce the amount of fresh air intake, and thus the cost of treating it. The effectiveness of these controls in museums and galleries is not known.

In winter, fresh air will be cold and so heating will be required. This is not an additional expense but an economy, since the amount of air to be heated is less than that which would have entered the building by natural ventilation. In old and historic buildings the method of getting this air in without unsightly ducting takes some ingenuity. In the Queen's House at the National Maritime Museum, plant was put in the roof space with the air passing to the rooms through the lined chimneys. Other plant was put in the basement and air supply grilles were located behind the radiators which were boxed in under the windows. The supply of conditioned air will create a positive pressure so that dirty external air is kept out; usually there is enough leakage to keep the pressure within comfortable limits. Pressure relief grilles normally deal with any excess.

Heating the air dries it, so additional humidity is required and can be added to the air in a variety of ways. Free-standing humidifiers are often used in smaller buildings and are used in the National Gallery for emergencies. Proper care and maintenance of these is labour intensive, so humidifying the supply air should be considered. In the National Gallery this is done mainly by steam injection into the supply ducts. Steam generators come in three main types. Those electrically heated like a kettle are simple but less responsive, so that in small spaces fluctuating demand is hard to control. Electrode boilers are responsive, but more attention to their maintenance is needed in hard-water areas. Both of these are normally local to the duct or plant into which the steam is injected. Where there is a large demand, centralised steam generators, whether electric or gas, can be advantageous in maintenance and control. Older plants use spray washers both to supply the humidification and wash out some of the pollution. To be effective in removing pollution, the sprays have to create a fine mist through which all the air flows. With spray washers, careful treatment of the water is needed to avoid bacterial growth. As the air leaves the spray chamber in a saturated condition it will have too much moisture. The humidity then has to be controlled by chilling the air to the required dew point and reheating to a suitable supply temperature, thus using significant amounts of energy.

Wherever humidification is used there will be a migration of moisture from the building. Apart from the loss with the air leaving the building, either as exhaust or leakage, there will be loss through the walls unless a perfect vapour barrier can be achieved. Since perfection is not possible, in most buildings a practical level of vapour sealing must be found and some vapour loss accepted. Window-glazing can have a significant impact on humidity levels. It is of no value injecting moisture into the air if it is removed through condensation forming on the windows. The building structure itself may restrict the permissible humidity level since condensation within the walls in cold weather could cause severe damage. Somerset House is an example of this problem as vapour sealing is difficult and timber baulks which are built into the walls are in danger if internal humidities of 54% relative humidity is maintained inside when the temperature outside is −4°C.

When selecting appropriate environmental conditions, the most significant action for energy conservation must be to deal with the deficiencies of the building. Only when that is done, as well as practicable, can the economies in heating, ventilation, and humidification be realised.

Where the quantity of sensitive material on display is limited and where the display design allows, conditioning an enclosure rather than the whole building merits consideration. Some large showcases in the British Museum and the Victoria & Albert Museum have been conditioned where conditioning the room was impossible.

Air-conditioning

Full air-conditioning is the ultimate in environmental control. It uses considerable energy so its design needs careful consideration. In a museum air-conditioning system, it is normal to have an 'all air' system so that there is no danger of water from the system leaking into the gallery. In this paper, a straightforward air-conditioning plant is discussed as it is more likely to be used in many small and medium-sized buildings than variable air volume and dual duct systems. The plant must handle an air flow sufficient to provide all the heating, cooling, humidifying or dehumidifying required.

A typical setup has an anti-frost heater in the fresh air intake followed by coarse particulate filters. From the mixing chamber, the correct ratio of fresh and recirculated air passes to the main plant where it is again filtered with fine particulate and carbon filters. If the humidity in the mixed air is too high it is chilled to remove excess moisture, then reheated to the temperature required for the gallery supply. If the humidity is too low then it is heated or cooled to the correct temperature and steam is added to make up the deficiency in moisture content.

An alternative older style of construction uses spray washers to wash the polluting gases out of the air and humidify it. Since the air then has a very high moisture content, it must then be chilled to dew point to remove the excess. It is then reheated to the supply temperature for the gallery. This system uses chilling and heating all year round, so it is not energy efficient. It does however have advantages in having inertia in its response which with simple controls can give reasonably good stability.

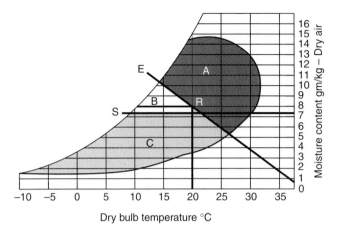

Figure 1 Psychrometric chart.

With a plant using steam humidification and modern controls it is possible to drive the plant for minimum energy consumption. The psychrometric chart (Fig. 1) shows the area within which weather conditions in the United Kingdom normally stay. In the diagram R represents the room conditions and S the supply absolute humidity. The exact level of the S line will vary with room heat and moisture gains. The line E is the room enthalpy (a measure of the energy in the air). The diagram is thus divided into three areas: A where the energy in the external air is greater than that returning from the room, B where the energy is less but the moisture greater than is needed in the supply air and C where both the moisture and the energy is less.

When external conditions fall into area A, any mixture of fresh air with the air recirculated from the room will increase the mixed-air energy level so only essential fresh air should be used to minimise the energy needed to treat the mixed air. In area B, any mixture of room and fresh air will have too high humidity and dehumidification is required. The fresh air has less energy so treating full fresh air under these conditions will be more efficient. Below line S, area C has less energy and moisture than the room air so a suitable ratio of room to external air will bring the mixture near to the S line and the additional heat and moisture must be supplied by the plant. Near the S line computation shows that it is more energy efficient to control the mixing of fresh and room air under the control of the temperature sensor, but in the area C, generally it is better to mix so that the humidity is as near correct as can be. To avoid complications in area C the humidity sensor should be in control.

The logic of a control system which will match these criteria is given in Figure 2. All references are to room temperature and humidity sensors, placed in as representative a position as possible. These must be the master control sensors for the system. The availability of reliable enthalpy measurement of external air makes the practical application possible and modern Building Management Systems have no difficulty in handling the logic.

Though the sensors in the room have overriding control, a simple feedback loop would not work as fluctuations in demand would lead to oscillations in the conditions due to the slow response time. Instead, more complex controls suited to the configuration of the system and its ductwork will require careful design and commissioning. The possibility of steam valves sticking and other equipment failures necessitates additional safety measures. It is safer to shut down the system and initiate an alarm than to try to compensate for equipment malfunction.

Whether the system adopted for a particular building is simple heating or a complex air-conditioning system, the importance of quality in the control system can not be exaggerated. There are plenty of good temperature sensors but there are still too many poor-quality humidity sensors available. For close control at ±4% relative humidity, sensors with a guaranteed accuracy of at least ±2% relative humidity are necessary and the characteristics of response time and hysteresis must be considered. The two types of humidity sensors which meet the standard are the electrolytic resistor type or some of the thin film capacitor types. It is the quality of control which defines the performance of the system, so money well spent on controls is never wasted.

In the National Gallery the assumption is that all sensors will fail or drift out of calibration with time, so a system of triple redundancy is used. This means that three sensors monitor each condition and the control system uses their outputs to find the pair of sensors in closest agreement. The average of these readings is used as the control parameter and the third sensor is checked to find out if its reading is similar to the others. If it is not, the alarm is raised and the sensor is recalibrated or replaced before it can affect the control of the system.

Lighting

Lighting is another environmental factor to be considered both for its direct effect on artifacts and as a load on the air-conditioning system. In Gallery 9 of the National Gallery tests were carried out to compare the lighting of the pictures using fluorescent tubes in parabolic reflectors, and two types of tungsten halogen lighting from tracks. While it was agreed

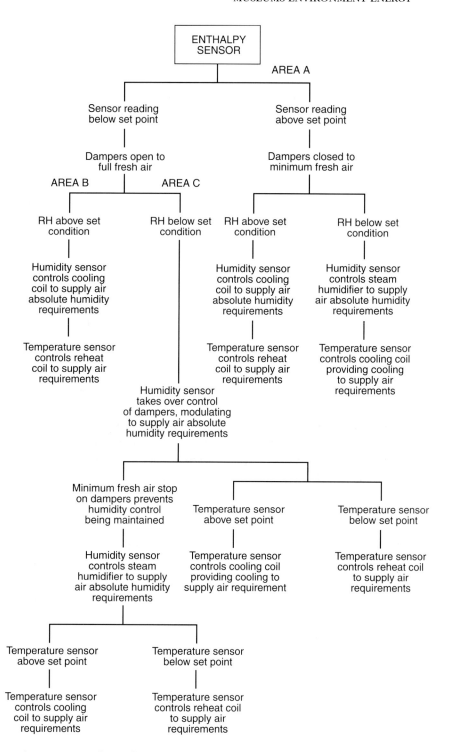

Figure 2 Control Logic for minimum energy.

that both gave good lighting, and the fluorescent fittings gave an clear even light, the Trustees decided that they preferred the 'sparkle' of the tungsten halogen. The initial and running costs of the lighting chosen is considerably higher than for fluorescent and the air-conditioning is also more heavily loaded.

Many galleries try to make good use of natural daylight, as in the National Gallery, where most rooms are top lit. The variability of daylight makes some form of active control desirable to protect the artifacts from light damage. While ultraviolet radiation is by far the most serious threat, all light can cause damage. In the National Gallery the target is to expose the paintings to not more than 600,000 lux hours per year with a UV level of less than 75 microwatts per lumen. With control of daylight comes a reduced load on the air-conditioning system.

The answer to the original question was 'Yes, to a degree and with difficulty'. This paper has attempted to show how the difficulties can be identified and dealt with in a way that is compatible with the building, the exhibits and the available funds.

Biography

Alfred Reading is a chartered engineer who has had long experience in research and development, production and design both in industry and in the Civil Service. He started his career with Ferranti Limited in Edinburgh and BICC Research Laboratories in London, before later joining the Air Ministry Works Department and later moving to MPBW on the Technical Secretariat of the ministerial committee on building maintenance.

In 1980 he became the Principal Engineer in the Property Services Agency's Museums and Galleries Group, London Region. He was responsible for team management of all the major engineering works of the group and supervised standards for engineering throughout the group. The buildings included the Kensington group of the Victoria & Albert Museum, the Natural History Museum and the Science Museum. The central group of the Tate Gallery, the National Gallery, the National Portrait Gallery and the Imperial War Museum, and a third group consisting of the British Museum, the Museum of Mankind and the National Maritime Museum. Much of the work involved the replacement of heating, ventilation and air-conditioning to upgrade standards. In some museums, air-conditioning replaced heating in some galleries. At the Tate Gallery, he was involved with the Clore Galleries and the development of the brief for the services in the Tate in the North at Liverpool. When the competition for the extension to the National Gallery was being organised, he wrote the engineering-services brief which was later modified for the Sainsbury Wing.

Between 1987 and 1991, he was Engineering Adviser to the National Gallery. In this role he advised on all the engineering aspects of projects, in particular he served on the liaison committee dealing with the Sainsbury Wing.

The National Gallery Sainsbury Wing Air-Conditioning System:
A Combination of Close Control and Energy Efficiency

Sean Ascough B Sc(Eng) MA CENG MIEI MCIBSE MIMechE Ove Arup & Partners Ireland

Introduction

In this paper I will describe the innovative air-conditioning system which has been designed and installed in the Sainsbury Wing to provide close control of air conditions in the picture areas. In particular I will focus attention on the hub of this system, which is its elaborate control system – one which has been made possible only by the advent of powerful computer-based building management systems (BMS).

Background

The solution which was decided upon has been moulded by several factors. Principally they are as follows:

1. Requirements of the brief:
     i. close environmental control
    ii. air cleanliness
   iii. reliability
    iv. maintenance
     v. energy efficiency

2. Project-related factors:
     i. building construction
    ii. architectural details
   iii. space
    iv. budget
     v. timescale

   The Sainsbury Wing is composed of a mixture of picture and non-picture areas. Picture areas include the main and temporary galleries as well as picture-packing and storage areas (Figs. 3, 4). The remainder of the building has been classified as a general area from the point of view of air-conditioning.

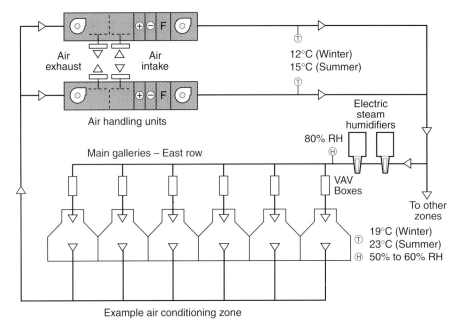

Figure 1 Simplified gallery air-conditioning schematic.

The purpose of using these two classifications was based on widely different environmental requirements. Since the gallery areas had more stringent requirements, such as closer control of temperature and humidity, greater air cleanliness and 24 hour rather than 10 hour operation, we made the decision to provide two separate air-conditioning systems: one for the gallery and one for the general areas. Thereby we avoided the unnecessary waste of over-conditioning the general areas.

This paper concentrates on the gallery air-conditioning system only. As the title suggests, I will approach this system from the aspect of close control and energy efficiency – two often conflicting attributes of a system.

It is necessary at this stage to emphasise that any reference I will make to energy efficiency will be relative to a conventional system with electric steam humidification. Close control air-conditioning systems are large users of energy and the Sainsbury Wing system is no exception. However, the use of various energy-efficient features in this system has meant a lower energy requirement than would otherwise be the case.

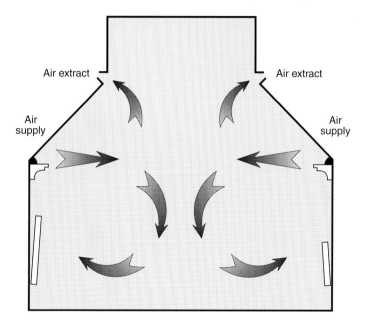

Figure 2 Air diffusion principle for typical gallery.

Gallery air-conditioning system

The system is broadly described as a variable air-volume (VAV) system. This means that the quantity of air passing through the system can be varied automatically to meet the building's current heating and cooling requirements. Such systems, commonly used in modern high-class office buildings, are generally noted for their energy efficiency and flexibility.

Figure 1 is a simplified schematic diagram of the gallery system. Working from outside inwards, there are air-intake and air-exhaust louvres which are connected to two parallel air handling units (AHUs). Sufficient fresh air for breathing by the occupants is taken into the system through these while an equivalent amount of stale air is dumped to the exterior. Each AHU has two fans: one for drawing air from the building and discharging some of it outside and the other for drawing air from outside and supplying air to the building. Also within each AHU is a means for regulating the ratio of fresh to recirculated air quantities, a heater and a cooler which are serviced with heating and chilled water respectively from the old gallery building and a bank of standard dust filters followed by activated carbon filters. These components unite to deliver air at constant temperature and free from dust and gases potentially hazardous to the collection.

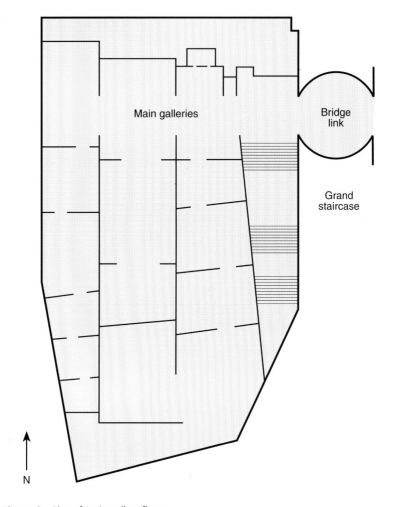

Figure 3 Plan of main gallery floor.

The AHUs operate in unison delivering air into a main air distribution duct. The air at this point has a constant temperature programmed to be between 12°C in winter and 15°C in summer. Branch ducts serving individual air-conditioning zones (of which there are seven) are fed from this main duct. Each zone has been selected on the basis that the area it covers have closely related load patterns and are located near each other.

Taking one zone, the east row of six main galleries, as an example; these six galleries are fed by one branch air duct fitted with a pair of electric resistance steam humidifiers incorporating 100% standby capacity. Air in the branch duct is humidified up to a constant relative humidity(RH) of 80%, the level required to maintain an RH of at least 50% in the galleries, where the temperature is considerably higher than in the duct. (It is important to remember that the RH of air decreases as its temperature increases).

Before air leaves its branch duct to serve a gallery in the zone, it passes through what is termed a VAV box where a final trimming control function is performed. The VAV boxes installed in the service walkways above the main galleries in the Sainsbury Wing consist of a motorised damper and an electric heater housed in an acoustically treated box. Electric heaters were selected rather than hot water ones due to the risk of water leakage on to paintings below. The motorised damper, in association with its own integral controls, regulates the air-flow to meet the needs of the gallery. If the gallery is too hot or dry, as sensed in the room itself, the air-flow rate is increased and vice versa if the gallery is too cool or humid. The heater is only called into action once the air-flow rate has been throttled to a minimum and it has a similar effect to reducing air-flow rate still further. The total of the VAV box air requirements throughout the duct network is met by varying the speeds of the fans in the two central AHUs. Finally, air enters the main picture galleries from a pair of opposing walls in each gallery via specially designed air diffusers tested in a laboratory mock-up. They are totally hidden from view by the architectural coving beneath them (Fig. 2). Spent air is extracted through architectural slots at high level and is ducted directly back to the central plant.

The principal energy-saving features offered by this particular solution are:

1. *Variable Fan Speeds* result in savings of electrical energy, i.e. only as much air as needed is moved.
2. *Full Free Cooling* is possible when outside conditions are favourable. This saves electrical energy associated with mechanical refrigeration.
3. *Single AHU Operation* is possible when the galleries are empty and lights are out.
4. *Inside Temperature Scheduling* between a nominal 19°C in winter and a nominal 23°C in summer saves energy on heating and humidification in winter and on refrigeration in summer.
5. *Large Humidity Control Zones* mean less standing heat losses from the reciprocally small number of humidifiers.

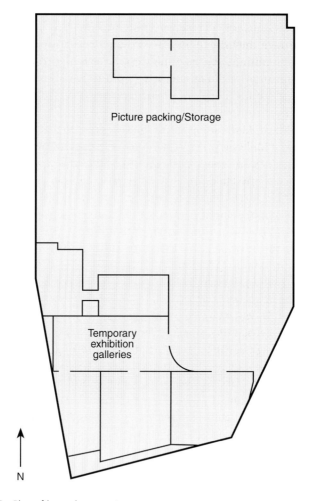

Figure 4 Plan of lower basement.

6. *BMS Monitoring* of all system parameters allows operators to examine trends and gives immediate report of any failures. Thus the system can be fine-tuned to be as efficient as possible and be easily maintained in effective operating order.

Building Management System (BMS)

The BMS is the indispensable controlling, co-ordinating and monitoring nerve-centre to which the viability and success of the gallery air-conditioning system must be attributed.

BMS systems are multipurpose microprocessor-based systems which can be installed and programmed to accept information from a wide variety of sources including air-conditioning systems. This information is processed through the logic of interlaced computer programs to give the desired output. Outputs can take the form of anything from a control signal for, for example, a fan to start to a graphical print-out of gallery air conditions for a twenty-four hour period.

Typical basic components which make up a BMS include a visual display unit (VDU), keyboard, printer, one or more computers(CPU) and interfaces to the building plant with interconnecting cablework. Various configurations of these components can be arranged depending on the nature and size of the building and its services. Many early BMS systems used a single CPU to deal with an entire building (Fig. 5). This had the disadvantages of large amounts of cabling and over-dependence on one CPU.

However, the most favoured solution today, and installed in the Sainsbury Wing, is to provide a number of smaller CPUs at various points around the building near to their related plant (Fig. 6). Each CPU is housed along with its ancilliary equipment in a unit termed an outstation (Fig. 7). This concept of distributed intelligence is made possible by networking the outstations together with a single twisted pair cable. A large number of signals can be transferred quickly through this communications link and is conducted by a process called token passing. In this way CPUs can effectively 'talk' to one another to give and receive data from different areas as required.

A BMS can be used as a centralised controlling and monitoring system for a wide range of building installations. In the Sainsbury Wing, for example, the BMS is also used to control the lighting systems.

Close control and energy efficiency through the BMS

Since the BMS is fundamentally driven by computer programmes, the scope of its application is limited by little other than the control engineer's ability to write such programmes, or software as they are often called. The need for many similar programmes comes up time and time again on different projects and so it is in the interest of BMS manufacturers that they develop standard, off-the-shelf software which can be easily replicated.

However, since all buildings are different and technology is ever marching forward, invariably the need will arise for special tailormade software to perform a certain design intention. In the Sainsbury Wing, a combination of standard and tailormade software has been used to achieve the objectives of reliability, close control and energy efficiency.

Located within maintenance engineers office

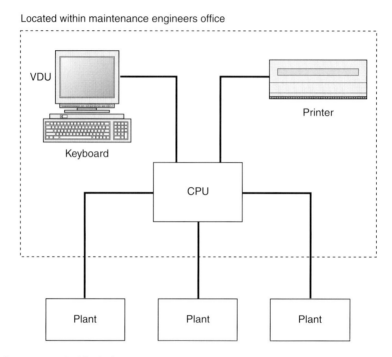

Figure 5 BMS with single CPU.

Examples of standard software

The examples of standard BMS software-driven control functions which contribute to close control and energy efficiency given here, could also have been performed by conventional solid state controls. However in this large project, they were best integrated into a BMS, particularly for ease of commissioning, monitoring and maintenance.

1. *Switching:* Switching functions are used for applications such as turning off chilled water pumps when there is no demand for chilled water.

2. *Timing:* Standard timing functions are used to orchestrate draindown of the electric steam humidifier boiling vessels at the ideal manufacturer-recommended frequencies. This can save on softened hot-water usage when compared to using electro-mechanical fixed cycle timers. Standard timing functions are also used to record the

number of hours for which plant has been running and thereby provide information useful for planned preventive maintenance.

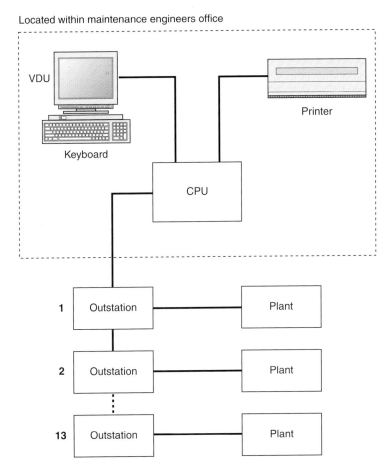

Figure 6   Sainsbury Wing BMS with networked outstations.

3. *Regulating:* Standard control functions are used to regulate the supply fan speeds to their (minimum) level required to sustain a fixed air pressure in the ductwork upstream of the VAV boxes (Fig. 8). The extract fan speeds are controlled by software which regulates them so that they draw back 85% of the air supplied. The balance of the air is used to help reduce air ingress from non-picture areas to picture

areas by producing a nett air-flow from the picture areas. In this way the picture areas are kept under positive pressure.

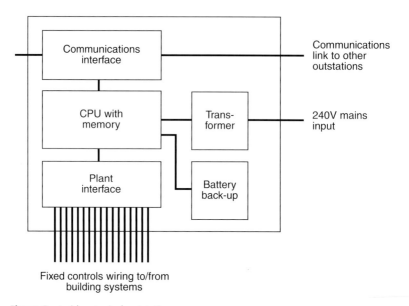

Figure 7   Inside a typical outstation.

Examples of project-specific software

Some examples of control routines which were especially prepared for the Sainsbury Wing air-conditioning system include:

1. *Software Governing Free Cooling:* As already described earlier, the two AHUs have the ability to take in variable amounts of fresh air from outside. When the building is occupied, a fixed minimum amount of air must always come from outside. However, certain conditions can exist when it is more beneficial to bring in all outside air rather than just a very small amount of it. Conversely, conditions also exist when this may not apply. Therefore in order to gain maximum benefit from the free cooling effect of outside air, a separate software algorithm was implemented in the BMS which only permits free cooling when it is both possible and economically viable to do so. The basic criteria embodied in the algorithm are represented graphically in the psychrometric chart (Fig. 9).

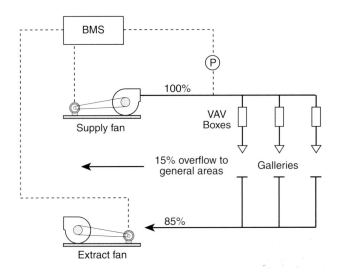

Figure 8 BMS control of fan speeds.

Free cooling is only permitted when outside conditions fall into the shaded area, which is approximately 30% of the time. Line A is determined by the capacity of the humidifier – which is designed for the minimum fresh air situation. Line B is generated by an ESHCO (Economical Steam Humidification Cycle with Optimisation) programme. An ESHCO programme can be defined as one which attempts to reconcile the potential increase in steam humidification load with the reduced need for refrigerated cooling associated with the use of cool outside air. Allowance is also made in the calculation here for the different ways in which the electrical energies being compared are used. In round figures, 1 kilowatt (kW) of electricity used in an electrical steam humidifier will give 1 kW worth of latent heat in steam whereas 1 kW of electricity fed into a refrigeration machine will typically give 3 kW worth of chilled water. Line C is a constant enthalpy or energy line. Outside air above this line has more thermal energy in it than the gallery air has. For this reason it cannot offer any cooling effect. The software governing free cooling is described in more detail in Appendix 1.

2. *Single AHU Operation:* In normal operation the two central AHUs deliver equal shares of the galleries' air needs. The total flow rate of air is directly related to the rate at which heat is being liberated into

the galleries by the lighting system and people. It will be at its lowest during the period when the Gallery is closed and the galleries are empty. In such instances the flow rate could be as low as 50% of its maximum of 20 metres^3 per second. So in order to exploit this fact the BMS has been used to sense if it is possible to switch off one AHU and so allow more efficient running on one well-loaded machine rather than on two lightly loaded ones. Energy is saved here through reduced heat loss from the variable fan speed motors, increased fan efficiency and switching off of an AHU secondary chilled water pump.

3. *Humidifier Control:* Working through the system towards the galleries, next comes the branch duct humidifiers. Their correct operation has a very important influence on maintaining general humidity levels in the galleries. Steam output is controlled through the BMS in response to humidity measurements from a high quality humidity sensor downstream of the humidifiers (Fig. 10). A second humidity sensor mounted beside the controlling sensor is used to provide a high humidity alarm, and, more interestingly, to provide a calibration check between the two sensors. If the two sensors disagree by more

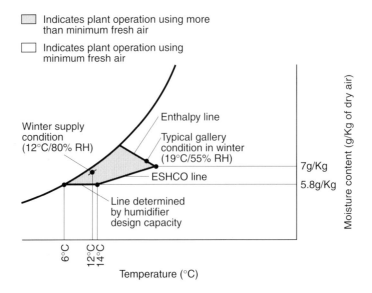

Figure 9 Constraints governing free cooling.

than 5% for one minute then an alarm is generated at the operator's station calling for their recalibration. Maintaining sensors in good calibration in such a manner obviously contributes to close control, but it also contributes to energy efficiency by avoiding wastage associated with overhumidifying.

4. *Room Temperature Adjustment:* In the Sainsbury Wing galleries there are two levels of room temperature adjustment. The first level is a broad seasonal one. Settings for the normal temperatures are adjusted between 19°C in winter and 23°C in summer by a software calculation within the BMS. During the spring and autumn the room temperatures are automatically adjusted at the rate of 0.25°C per week (Fig. 11). As mentioned before, this gives an inside environment which is more sympathetic to outside conditions and contributes to energy efficiency.

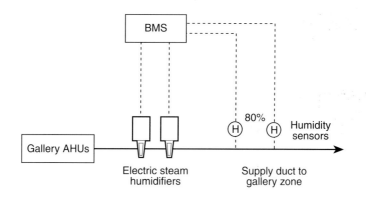

Figure 10   Gallery zone RH control.

The second level is a finer level of adjustment aimed specifically at conservation of the collection. It uses temperature adjustment to limit the extent and rate of humidity variations in the galleries. Such variations may be caused by different usage patterns of the galleries. Temperature control in each gallery is conducted by the BMS and takes the form outlined in Figure 12. This drawing is based on a psychrometric chart and illustrates operating parameters for winter time. The BMS controls the VAV boxes to meet the instantaneous required room temperature. If the room humidity has somehow fallen to 50% (its lowest allowable level) then the room temperature will be dropped from its usual 19°C, down to 18°C, in order to help

increase the humidity. Between 52% and 58% room RH the temperature is held at its 19°C mid-band by a combination of proportional
and integral control actions. If latent heat emissions from visitors
should cause the gallery humidity to exceed 58% then the room
temperature is scheduled upwards towards 20°C. This has the effect
of reducing the speed at which the humidity increases and it also
reduces the extent to which it does.

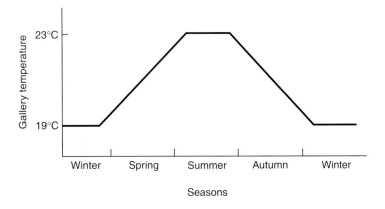

Figure 11 Seasonal adjustment of gallery temperature.

If the humidities of all the galleries in a given zone exceed 58%
then the duct humidity is automatically dropped. Its normal level is
reinstated once all the gallery RHs in the zone have dropped below
58% again. When compared to a conventional system having individual humidifier settings for each gallery, this method of control has
distinct advantages in terms of capital cost, space requirements,
energy usage and maintenance.

5. *Triple Redundancy (TR):* The gallery room temperatures and
    humidities just mentioned are both single discrete values which have
    been derived through a triple redundancy calculation executed by
    BMS. Taking the RH value, for example, three individual RH sensors
    are used to measure ambient RH at picture level in the galleries. RH
    values from each of these three sensors are analysed by the BMS to
    determine which pair is in closest agreement. The triple redundancy
    RH value used for control purposes is then the average of this sensor
    pair. The third sensor is disregarded completely. However, if it
    disagrees with the other two by more than a set amount, an alarm

calling for sensor recalibration is generated at the BMS operator's station.

The main effective advantage of the TR method is an increased and more maintainable level of measurement accuracy, not to mention reliability than that afforded by a single sensor.

Smoke-extract system

A mechanical smoke-extract system has been installed to clear smoke from within the Sainsbury Wing in the event of a fire. The system is a mechanical rather than a natural one, since the large building openings associated with a naturally ventilated system would have conflicted with the Gallery's environmental and security requirements. Its objectives are to help people escape from a fire, to aid fire-fighting and to help minimise smoke damage to the collection.

It is the only ventilation system in the building which is not controlled by BMS. For safety reasons, and at the request of the District Surveyor for Westminster, the area in which the National Gallery is located, the building's smoke-extract system had to be controlled in a conventional hard-wired manner. This means that all of the controls directly pertaining to the operation of the smoke-extract system had to be assembled from physical wiring, relays and other equipment.

The system itself consists of three identical smoke-extract fans. These are connected into the normal building extract system which has been fire protected to give it a dual air and smoke extract function. In normal operation, the smoke-extract fans are isolated from the building ductwork by motorised dampers. In a fire situation these dampers open while two other dampers close in order to isolate the AHUs. Two smoke-extract fans of three are used together to draw smoke from the building and discharge it to outside. If one should fail, the third fan starts automatically to take its place.

Performance testing of gallery air-conditioning system

After the normal commissioning and balancing stage of the project, a range of performance testing activities were devised prior to the hanging of the collection. The main purpose of these tests was to prove that the control system had been tuned to cater for changing load conditions.

Among the tests was one for simulated gallery design occupancy. Thermal loads in the permanent picture galleries were simulated by arrays of 100-watt General Lighting Service (GLS) lamps distributed evenly about each gallery, each lamp representing the sensible heat of one person. Latent heat from each person was simulated by electric kettles wired through variax transformers set up to give latent loads equivalent to 60 watt per person. These artificial loads along with the normal house lighting allowed realistic modelling of the air-conditioning system performance. It was also the only practical way of providing the information needed to allow fine-tuning of the control system's response to a unique air-conditioning system in a unique space with unique thermal influences. Throughout the testing there was a continuous monitoring and recording done of all relevant signals to and from the BMS.

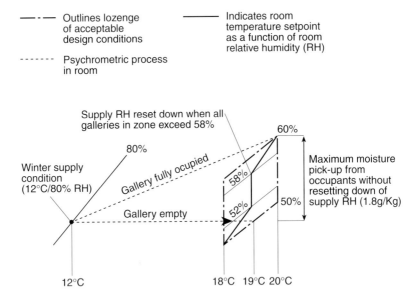

Figure 12 Trimming control at galleries – wintertime example.

Fine-tuning of the control parameters, as a result of these tests, allowed closer control of conditions coupled with the minimum amount of energy needed to achieve them. For this reason, it is strongly recommended that such tests should be considered on almost every project where close control is needed, especially where a BMS is involved.

Biography

Sean Ascough studied building services engineering at the College of Technology, Dublin. In 1988 he joined Ove Arup & Partners as an HVAC Design Engineer. He was Project HVAC Engineer on the National Gallery's Sainsbury

Wing project from spring 1989 until its opening in the summer of 1991. Among the design and supervisory activities, his work included directing a set of air-conditioning plant performance tests. Following this, he designed a chilled water system for the Gulbenkian Hall Art Galleries at the Royal College of Art, London. In September 1991 he transferred to Ove Arup & Partners, Ireland.

Appendix 1

Algorithm to govern fresh air quantity into gallery AHUs

1. General

Depending on internal and external temperature and humidity conditions, the amount of outside air admitted to the system can be varied to provide the most economical mode of operation.

The algorithm illustrated in Figure 13, and followed in the point by point narrative below, is essentially a filter placed in the supply temperature control logic leading to damper modulation for free cooling.

This 'filter' is two-stage. The first stage determines whether humidification is necessary to bring the air to its required supply condition. If it is necessary then the amount of steam needed is compared to the design limits for maximum and minimum fresh air volumes. Should either limit be exceeded, the AHUs immediately take protective action by shutting down to a lower fresh air quantity. Monitoring of gallery relative humidity and humidifier output signals represents a cross-check of this action.

Thus, having determined whether or not free cooling is possible, the second ESHCO stage (Economical Steam Humidification Cycle with Optimisation) assesses the economic viability of free cooling by taking a basic electric steam humidification to refrigerated cooling cost ratio of 3.

Free cooling (and enthalpy control) can then commence if these two stages are satisfied, that is, free cooling is both possible and desirable.

2. BMS Programme Points and Narrative

A. Points 1 to 9 marked on Figure A are read for information:

1. Building Occupancy Schedule:
The mode of building occupancy (that is, whether the building is open or closed to visitors) is used here to determine whether the AHUs should at least deliver their design minimum quantity of fresh air. This quantity corresponds to 23% of the design volume of 20 metres^3 per second. Therefore the air handling plant can be run automatically without any fresh air input when the building is closed and the economics so dictate.

2. Manual Damper Recirculation:
The normal configuration of the AHUs mixing dampers can be manually overridden to any position. They will remain in that position until the signal is manually removed. This function will be especially useful in the event of humidifier failure or isolation for maintenance.

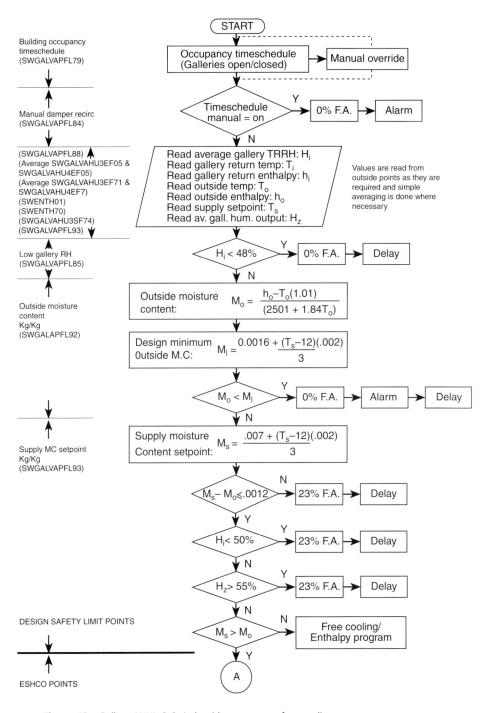

Figure 13 Gallery AHU's 3 & 4 algorithm to govern free cooling.

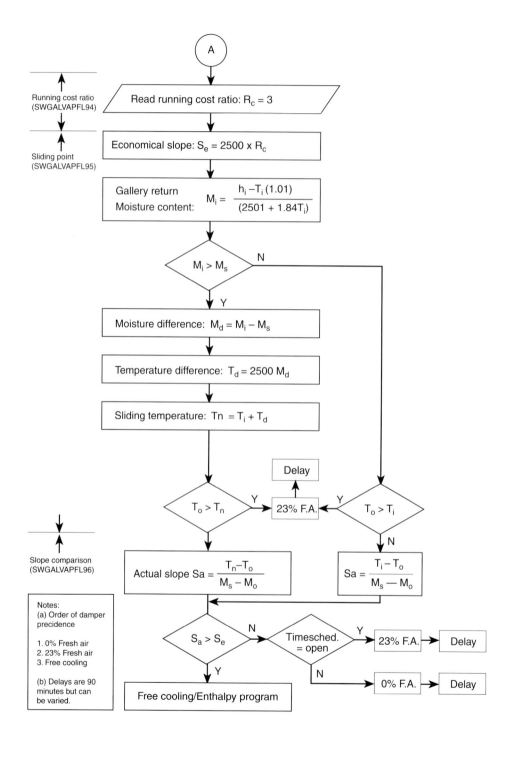

3–9. Points Numbered 3 to 9:

The current values of these points are read into the design safety limits points and the ESHCO points as and where required. Simple averaging is done locally where necessary.

B.   Points 10 to 12 indicate the Design Safety Limit:

10. Low Gallery RH:

Should the average value of the galleries triple redundancy RH readings fall below 48% then the plant goes into a total recirculation mode. It will remain in this mode for a minimum period of 90 minutes.

11. Outside Moisture Content:

The actual outside moisture content is calculated using the standard enthalpy equation. Advantage is taken of the precalculated outside enthalpy value. In effect the known sensible component is deducted thus allowing the moisture content to be ascertained.

The design minimum outside moisture content for the time of year is calculated. For wintertime this has a value of .0016kg/kg and is illustrated on Figure 14 by the line AA. This line moves upwards as summertime approaches and eventually reaches a maximum level of .0036kg/kg, line BB.

If the outside moisture content drops below its design minimum the plant will revert to total recirculation for at least 90 minutes. An alarm is also raised to inform the operator of the severity of the outside conditions.

12. Supply Moisture Content Setpoint:

The supply moisture content setpoint for the time of year is calculated based on a scheduled supply temperature between 12°C and 15°C from winter to summer and an approximately constant supply RH of 80%.

Moisture content variation is represented by the line CC. Within this point, four different checks are made to ascertain that the air handling plant is operating within the normal design limits of the humidifiers:
i. If the difference between supply and outside air moisture contents is greater than the design maximum moisture addition of a single humidifier at full air volume, the plant must revert to minimum fresh air operation.

The minimum outside moisture content line below which free cooling is not allowed is represented by the line DD. This line follows the scheduled supply moisture content with a constant difference of .0012kg/kg.
ii. If the average gallery triple redundancy RH drops below 50%, the plant reverts to minimum fresh air operation.

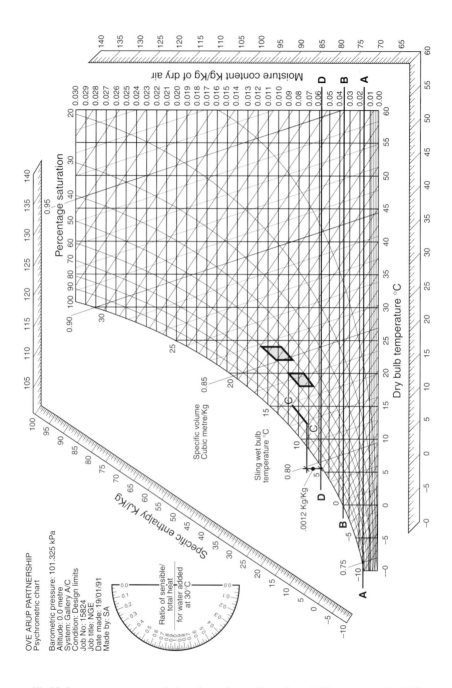

iii. If the average control signal to the gallery humidifiers exceeds 55% (allowing for one humidifier draining down at once) it is deemed that too much outside air of too low a moisture content is being handled. The plant therefore reverts to minimum fresh air operation.

iv. If the moisture content setpoint of the supply air is greater than the outside moisture content, it is deemed that some level of humidification is necessary. In such a case, the subsequent ESHCO part of the software will have a bearing on whether the plant operates on free cooling. If no humidification of the outside air is necessary, the control emphasis can shift to the free cooling and enthalpy control programme.

This routine is the last of the design safety limit checks before the ESHCO programme.

C. Points 13 to 15 are the ESHCO programme:

13. Running Cost Ratio:

This point allows the operator to select a kilowatt for kilowatt cost ratio between the cost of electrical steam humidification and the cost of cooling by mechanical refrigeration. Initially this ratio has been set as 3:1, based on an average chiller coefficient of performance of 3, all other costs assumed as being of an equal ratio. This ratio may be easily changed in the future if experience indicates differently.

14. Sliding Point:

For any given running cost ratio, a line can be drawn on the psychrometric chart (see Fig. 15, Line FA) from the return air condition in the direction of decreasing temperature. This line can have such a slope that, in the regime of cooling and humidification, it is more cost-effective to humidify and cool a marginal kilogram of outside air lying above the line, than to simply cool a marginal kilogram of air at the exhaust condition.

That is to say free cooling with large quantities of fresh air is more cost-effective for outside air conditions above the line and minimum fresh air is more cost-effective for outside conditions below the line. The slope of this dividing line is termed the economical slope.

The next feature of the programme uses a calculation of the gallery return moisture content to ascertain the extent to which the galleries are latently loaded. Moisture pickup in excess of the supply moisture content setpoint is converted to an artificially increased gallery return temperature on the basis of the constant enthalpy line BC. This causes the upper point of the economical slope line to slide in the direction of increasing temperature and so expanding the opportunities for free cooling.

As an example, the inside air condition can be taken as B and the outside air as D. The algorithm therefore considers that the cost of latently cooling a marginal kilogram of inside air from B to F, and then sensibly cooling it to G, is the same as humidifying a marginal kilogram of outside air from D to E, and then sensibly cooling it to G.

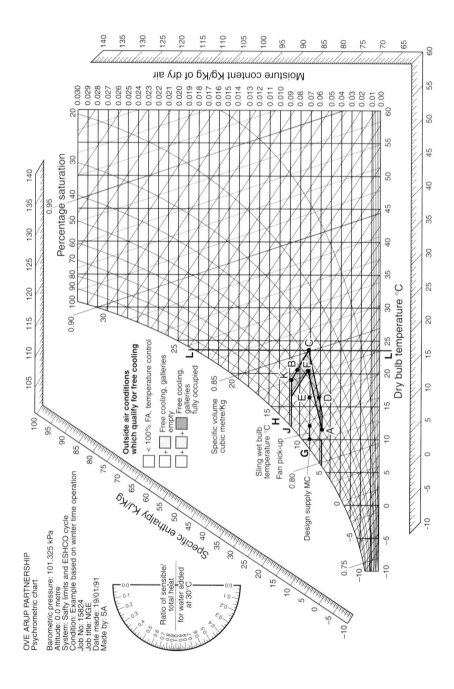

The same principles apply for outside air conditions which are below 10°C, but the amount of fresh air taken then would be dictated by the off AHU temperature control.

The lines HC and JK are enthalpy and high moisture content changeover thresholds to give more cost-effective and favourable off-coil conditions than would otherwise be achieved using outside air in conditions above them.

Outside air with temperatures in excess of the sliding point temperature (above the line LL) are committed to minimum fresh air since it is not cost-effective to cool and/or humidify such air.

15. Slope Comparison:
The final point in the ESHCO programme determines whether a given outside condition has the potential to allow economical free cooling.

A comparison is made between the economically sloped line and the actual line pertaining to a particular outside condition and sliding-point condition. This tells on which side of the economical line the outside condition lies. If it lies above the line then free cooling can commence to the dictates of the standard enthalpy control programme, all other conditions having been satisfied. If it lies below the line then the plant reverts to its minimum allowable fresh air level; 23% during opening hours and 0% after hours.

Throughout the algorithm described here, the hierarchy of damper positions is in the order: 0% fresh air, 23% (minimum) fresh air and free cooling/enthalpy control. Also the assembly of points and dividing lines illustrated in Figure 15 will automatically shift up and down on the chart depending on the gallery design conditions for the time of year considered.

Lighting Design and Energy Efficiency in Museums and Galleries

Michael Carver B.Tech(Hons) C.Eng MCIBSE The Steensen Varming Mulcahy
Partnership

Summary

There are many factors that need to be taken into account when considering new or refurbished lighting designs for museums and galleries. This
paper first looks at the deleterious effects of light before identifying the
importance of daylight as an energy-efficient light source. Properly integrated with artificial lighting, it can contributes significantly to reductions
in lighting energy costs.

Following a review of the performance of a number of energy-
efficient light sources the paper presents case-study material in relation to
a number of refurbished gallery spaces.

Introduction

Lighting design is fundamental to any museum or art gallery, for it is with
light that objects are seen. However it was David Saunders of the National
Gallery who said that 'our starting point is that any light must be seen as a
concession'. Fortunately the needs of museum collections and those of
energy conservation go very much hand-in-hand, but it is necessary to
balance the quantity of light with the needs of visitors who wish to view
objects in a manner that is both informative and aesthetically pleasing.

Deleterious effects of light

It is possible to group objects into three basic categories according to their
sensitivity to light:

1. Works that contain no organic material which are therefore insensi-
    tive to the action of light. Examples include ceramics and objects
    made from stone, metal, glass and enamel.
2. Works which are partially sensitive to the action of light in that they
    contain organic substances or organic substances which are protected
    in some way. Examples of works in this class include oil painting which

    contain pigments derived from organic origins, but where the oil medium offers a degree of protection.

3.   Works which are especially sensitive to light because they contain unprotected organic substances. Examples include textiles, drawings and manuscripts using pastels, water colours, or inks.

The extent of the deterioration depends upon a number of factors:

1.   The intensity of light.
2.   The time exposure.
3.   The spectral characteristic of the light.
4.   The intrinsic capacity of individual organic substances to absorb and be affected by light.

External factors also influence the rate of deterioration:

    1.   Humidity.
    2.   Temperature.
    3.   Active gasses present in the atmosphere (sulphur dioxide and oxygen in particular).

High temperature and high relative humidity speed up the process of photodecomposition as well as causing the more generally recognised forms of physical deterioration. At normal temperatures and humidity, however, the rate of change of temperature and humidity is usually of more concern.

    Oxidation of colours brought about by the action of light is the principal chemical reaction associated with fading and the presence of oxygen will speed this process. In practice it is not possible to exclude oxygen below the few parts per million necessary and therefore exposure to light must be controlled.

    Taking the intensity of light together with exposure, the principle of reciprocity states that the cumulative photochemical effect is proportional to the result of the product of intensity and time. If D is the relative damage factor, I the intensity and t the time of exposure it follows that:

$$D = K_1 \, (I \times t)$$

Where K_1 is a function of cumulative damage.

    The damage brought about by the action of light is cumulative, and as the rate of fading commonly decreases with exposure, to the point where no further fading occurs, it is not possible to say that the level of exposure is directly proportional to the amount or rate of fading.

    However, when the relative amount of light damage is low, it is possible to assume as a general rule of thumb that the amount of fading is proportional to exposure to light. Any error here will be in favour of the longer-term preservation of the item in question.

Thus 200 lux exposure for one hour is going to do as much damage as 100 lux exposure for two hours. The reciprocity principle, or total exposure theory, has been found to hold reasonably well in the fading of modern dyed textiles throughout a fifty-fold range in intensity[1] and another study[2] of more than 1,000 samples reported only 4% of cases where the rule did not hold true.

Dealing with the spectral composition of light, the shorter the wavelength the greater the energy of the photon. Therefore the shorter wavelengths of visible and ultraviolet light, the more photochemically potent the action of light is likely to be. The relative damage factor has been found[3] to be inversely proportional to the log of the wavelength (λ):

$$D = k_2 \cdot \log \frac{1}{\lambda}$$

where K_2 is a function of the material.

From this equation it can be seen that light at the ultraviolet end of the spectrum with its short wavelength is most harmful and should be avoided. Figure 1 shows that daylight has a high ultraviolet component and therefore direct exposure of objects to daylight should be avoided.

Relative power per unit wavelength

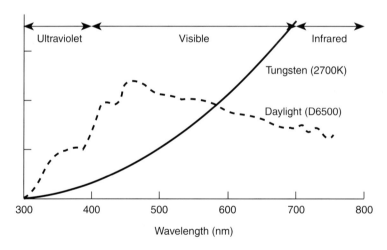

Figure 1a Relative spectral power of daylight, and tungsten light sources.

Daylight design

Whilst daylight has a high proportion of ultraviolet content it is very often the preferred light source for aesthetic reasons. From an energy conservation viewpoint it should be used to the greatest possible extent, as daylight is often readily available for a large proportion of gallery opening hours.

Relative power per unit wavelength

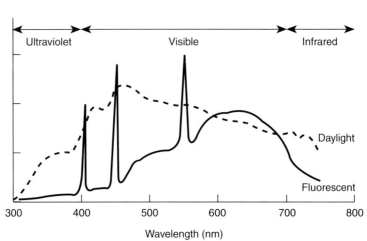

Figure 1b Relative spectral power of daylight and colour 93 fluorescent lamps.

Designing for the successful use of daylight however is complex and often model-testing in an artificial sky is the only way of predicting in advance the likely performance of any given geometric arrangement. To overcome ultraviolet penetration there are a number of approaches that can be adopted:

1. Arrange for all daylight entering the space to be reflected once before entering the space housing sensitive objects.
2. Apply ultraviolet filtering films to the window glazing.
3. Apply ultraviolet filtering films to glass barriers providing physical protection for objects.

Films designed for application to glass have improved significantly in recent years and sometimes films designed for solar heat gain control and security protection have excellent UV absorbing qualities. However, the application of a film, particularly externally, often gives rise to misgivings about durability and long-term performance and therefore, if possible, geometric arrangements providing a once reflected route are to be preferred.

In most galleries the only reasonable way to introduce daylight to the space is to use top lighting and even with designs that utilise one or more reflections to transfer daylight to the hanging zone, it is possible that daylight factors in excess of 1% will be achieved. With external levels potentially rising to 90,000 lux it can be seen that a method of control is required to minimise excessive daylight penetration during summer and maximise levels towards the end of the day during winter.

The Clore Gallery for the Turner collection utilises[4] a system of wide blade external louvres designed to moderate daylight penetration. Rather than continuously responding to an internal photocell which would provide a rather bland constant light level, the blades are set to a preset position for each hour of the day taking into account sun position in the sky, and left unaltered until the next hour. In this way the natural variations of daylight are reflected internally whilst at the same time minimising overall exposure. External louvres can also be used to achieve the reflected route for UV protection, even if the roof geometry is not suitable. By using a control system that calculates sun position on a continuous basis, it is possible to exclude direct sun penetration but permit entry of light reflected from the louvres themselves.

Artificial light sources

In selecting lamps for the display of objects there are many considerations to be taken into account, not least the efficiency of the lamp in producing light from electrical input:

   i. Lumen output per watt of electrical input (efficacy).
   ii. Spectral composition of the light produced.
   iii. Colour rendering performance.
   iv. Shape and size of the lamp and the possibilities for focusing and controlling the light.
   v. Lamp life.

There are many differing light sources and the relative lumen efficiencies of each group are given in Figure 2. Discharge sources have not tradition-ally been suitable for use in museums and galleries due to poor colour-rendering properties and often excessive lumen output. However small and lower wattage discharge lamps are now available with acceptable colour-rendering properties. It can also be seen from Figure 2 that overall efficacies vary significantly from about 15 lumens per watt for general lighting service (GLS) tungsten lamps to just under 100 lumens per watt for high-frequency fluorescent lighting.

Colour rendering

Whilst the spectral content of a light source is important, particularly in the area of ultraviolet content, the ability to render colours of surfaces accurately is also important. The definition of what is 'accurate' is quite difficult in that daylight, the first consideration for comparison, varies significantly in spectral content and hence colour-rendering properties vary with time of day, time of year, and weather conditions. The Commission International de l'Eclairage (CIE) has established a general colour-rendering index using a set of 8 test colours. This is referred to as R_a8 or just R_a. A more complex standard uses 16 colours (R_a16). The index is based on the accuracy with which these test colours are reproduced as judged by a panel of testers by the lamp of interest compared to a standard tungsten light source. Perfect agreement is given a value of 100. For museums and galleries, and indeed office environments, we are usually only interested in lamps with colour-rendering indices in excess of 80.

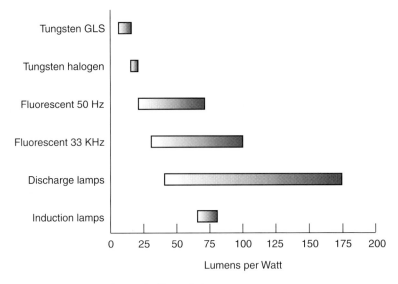

Figure 2 Luminous efficacy of differing light sources.

In addition the colour temperature measured in degrees Kelvin is used as a measure of the resulting ambience or feel, and is a measure of the apparent colour of the light. The CIE identify 3 colour temperature groups:

Warm :	below 3300K
Intermediate :	between 3300K and 5300K
Cold :	above 5300K

Tungsten lighting is generally warm, whilst fluorescent lighting can be obtained in a range of colour temperatures. Daylight varies from a colour temperature of 2,000K at sunrise and sunset to 5,500K with normal midday sun and beyond up to 10,000K with blue skies reflected on snow.

If restoration and retouching of repairs are undertaken then it is vital to consider the light source used. If it differs from the light used for general viewing, then repairs which were a perfect match during restoration can become very obvious with even just a slight shift in colour rendering. Successful restoration under all viewing conditions requires a full understanding of the colourants involved so that the appropriate compromises can be made.

Light sources for efficient lighting design

Tungsten light sources, and particularly low-voltage tungsten halogen, are very attractive sources of light in a number of respects. They tend to be compact and available in a wide variety of forms with the possibility of close control focusing into wide angle or narrow beam widths. In addition they are easily dimmed, do not require control circuitry, they also have a continuous spectrum and good colour rendering. However there are a number of key disadvantages. The primary disadvantage is low luminous efficiency leading to high installed loads for a given illumination level, high running costs and also leading to the possibility of overheating or a requirement for additional air-conditioning capacity which itself leads to higher running costs. Additionally low-voltage tungsten halogen lamps with the quartz enclosure unprotected by glass have a very high ultraviolet component as quartz is almost transparent to UV light. With very short life, usually 1,000 hours maximum and often much shorter for low-voltage tungsten halogen, reliability is poor and replacement costs high.

Fluorescent lighting, because of its improved output compared with tungsten sources (Fig. 2), is therefore an obvious choice where improved efficiency is required and where high uniformity ratios are essential.

Traditional fluorescent lighting control gear has utilised a wire-wound choke and has been operated at mains frequency. Newer electronic ballasts operate at higher frequencies in the range 28–41 KHz, and, in addition to increasing the lamp efficiency (Fig.3), have much reduced losses within the ballast resulting in up to 30% power-saving compared with traditional control gear. There are many other advantages, and within galleries the ability to dim high-frequency controlled fluorescent lighting with a small number of passive components is very attractive.

The advantages of high-frequency control gear and lamps are:
  i. Up to 30% power-saving compared to traditional control gear.
  ii. Mains flicker eliminated.
  iii. Low sensitivity to variations in mains voltage.
  iv. Improved lamp life.
  v. Reliable and quick starting even in cold conditions.

vi. Power factor near unity.

vii. Regulation of output between 10 and 100% is possible with minimum additional equipment.

viii. Reduction in weight.

ix. Audible noise and vibration eliminated.

There is an ever-increasing variety of fluorescent lamps to choose from. Samples from the range offered by Philips are classified by lumen efficiency in Figure 4. Other manufacturers, notably Thorn, Siemens and Woton, all produce similar ranges. As can be seen lumen efficacy per watt ranges from about 72 to 98 lumens/watt for the colour 80 series lamps which achieves a colour-rendering index (R_a8) of 85. Tubes are available at colour temperatures of approximately 3000K (the warm end of intermediate) and 4000K (the cool end of intermediate).

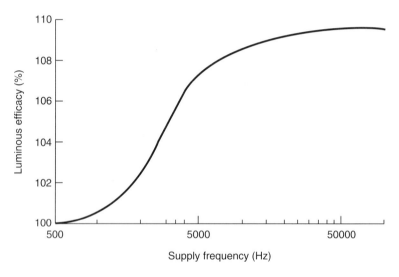

Figure 3 Luminous efficacy of fluorescent tubes with variable frequency supply.

If very much better colour rendering is required, the colour 90 series of tubes provides a colour-rendering index (R_a8) of 95 with the added advantage that they have a very much lower spectral content below 400 nm (the ultraviolet region). The design lumens per watt, however, are significantly reduced leading to higher energy consumption for the same level of illuminance. Unless there is an overriding concern for improved colour-rendering, the colour 80 series of tubes is a good compromise between energy efficacy and colour-rendition. Fluorescent tubes with good colour rendering characteristics are quite expensive compared with general purpose tubes with typical retail prices for a 1,500mm colour 80 series lamp being about £6.80 and £8.00 for a colour 90 series.

Low-frequency fluorescent tubes have a nominal life of about 9,000 hours which equates to approximately 3 years' use in a gallery with little or no daylight contribution. High-frequency control circuits, however, are much kinder to the tubes and manufacturers are quoting about 12,000 hours life although it is possible that 15,000 hours life will be achieved in practice. With the high cost of replacement this extended life is a very real benefit.

New developments in discharge lighting are producing lamps suitable for accent and top-up lighting in museums and galleries. The white SON lamp has an efficiency of 40 lumens/watt with a colour-rendering index of 80%. The colour appearance is warm and closely matches tungsten light but with a four-fold increase in efficiency and a life-expectancy of about 4 to 5 times, it reduces significantly relamping costs. A 35 watt white SON lamp is equivalent in output to a 140 watt GLS lamp.

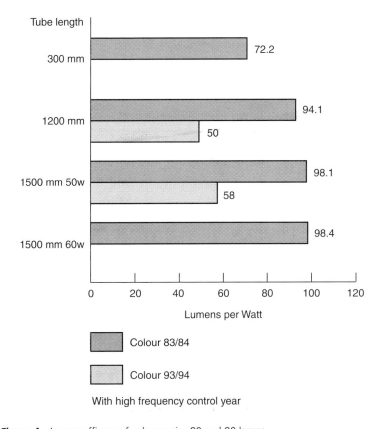

Figure 4   Lumen efficacy of colour series 80 and 90 lamps.

Another interesting discharge lamp is the single-ended metal halide. Again the colour-rendering index is 80% but the lumen output rises to 70 lumens/watt. This particular lamp combines a twin glass envelope with ultraviolet filtration to almost eliminate UV below 420nm. The lamp has a colour temperature of about 4,000K and is cooler in appearance than the white SON but would mix well with colour 84 or 94 tubes. A useful feature of this lamp is the very small light source area (about 7mm square) which makes it very suitable for use with focusing optics. At present, however, there are few luminaires available which exploit this potential.

A very recent development is the induction discharge lamp and this is exciting for its life potential which is in excess of 80,000 hours or more than 20 years operation! Luminous efficiencies about 70 lumens/watt are expected with good colour-rendering characteristics and the possibility of dimming in the future.

Lighting control and maintenance

If full advantage of daylight is to be made, it is essential that artificial lighting is properly controlled. There are a number of systems on the market specifically designed for use in galleries that not only control the switching of the lighting to minimise its use but also dim the lighting in response to daylight levels, linked through photocell detection.

The description of these systems is beyond the scope of this paper but if such systems are considered, it is essential that they are kept simple in concept and in operation. The marginally improved performance of sophisticated systems can be more than offset by lack of understanding by those with day-to-day operational responsibilities, and in addition more complex systems, can be prone to more frequent failure or calibration difficulties.

Having installed a new lighting system it is essential to maintain as far as possible the original performance by regular and adequate mainten-ance. As fluorescent tubes age, so their lumen output declines. After an initial rapid drop of 2 or 3% there is a steady decline until electrical failure occurs. This is demonstrated in Figure 5 where it can be seen that traditional halophosphate tubes have a significantly higher reduction with age than the new triphosphor tubes. High-frequency operation again gives a significant improvement over low frequency operation.

In addition there will be a steady reduction in output due to soiling of the lamp reflectors and diffusers surfaces. Cleaning (Fig. 6) can restore levels back to the lumen depreciation curve for the tube. If the space is overlit by about 20 to 30% based on the initial design lumens it is possible for a dimming system to compensate for the variation in output with time to ensure that a constant level is achieved. In practice, however, automatic dimming systems can be difficult to set up and calibrate and simplicity of operation should be sought wherever possible.

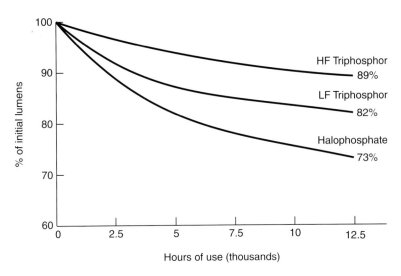

Figure 5 Lumen maintenance with age for fluorescent tubes.

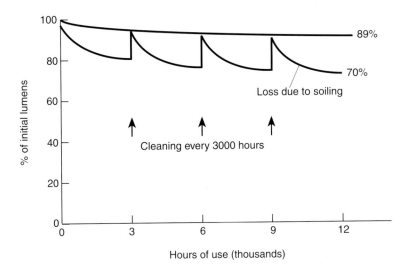

Figure 6 Light output depreciation with cleaning every 3,000 hours.

Case studies

The Steensen Varming Mulcahy Partnership are involved in the design of engineering services, including lighting, for a number of important museums and galleries. A review is provided of some recent work giving key design information to enable readers to adopt solutions to their own circumstances. Generally art galleries are considered here, and in addition to providing installed loads as a measure of likely energy consumption in terms of watts/m^2 of floor area, installed loads in terms of watts/m^2 of long area are also given. If existing galleries are encountered that are lit perhaps with track mounted PAR 38 tungsten lamps, then comparison of installed loads with those given here will indicate the potential savings possible by redesigning the installations with a more efficient light source. If in addition galleries are top lit, and daylight-linked controls are incorporated, then further savings in the order of 50% to 60% can be expected as the quantity of daylight available during gallery opening hours is significant. The shading in Figure 7 indicates the proportion of the year where external illuminance exceeds 10,000 lux during gallery opening hours of 10.00am to 6.00pm. This is about 70% of opening hours and with a top-lit gallery 10,000 lux externally will normally provide adequate levels on hanging walls, requiring a 1% daylight factor to produce a 100 lux internally.

Gallery 9, Tate Gallery, London

This traditional gallery at the Tate Gallery was refurbished and relit in 1988 utilising energy-efficient high-frequency luminaires and has an installed load in the order of 26 watts per m^2 of floor area. This drops to about 15 watts per m^2 of hanging area on the basis that hanging could take place up to the cornice (Fig. 8).

The new lighting system consists of 4 rows of twin 1,500mm, 50 watt, colour 83 high-frequency lamps in a metal reflector fitting giving a batwing distribution. Wedge-shaped cross blades are used to limit glare when looking down the gallery. In addition simple batten fittings (rows 3 & 6 in Fig. 9) are used to provide uplight on the ceiling which shows off the magnificent proportions of this gallery which is approximately 11.7m high. In practice very even illumination of the hanging zone is achieved largely due to rows 2 & 5 and in practice rows 1 & 4 which tend to light the floor are dimmed to a much lower level reducing power requirements.

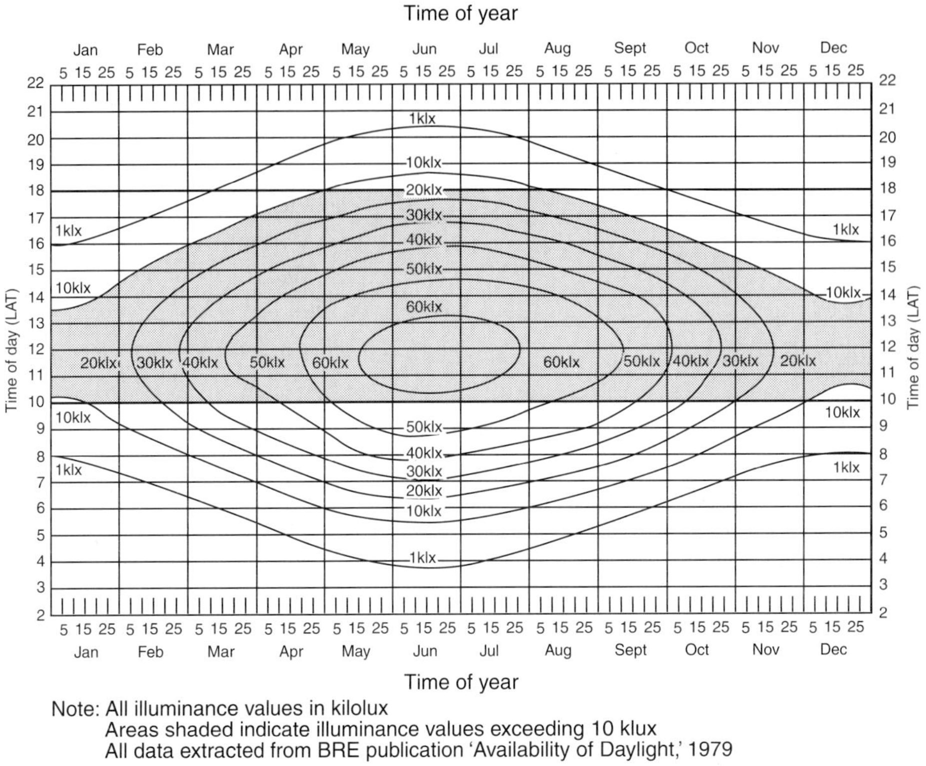
Time of year
Jan Feb Mar Apr May Jun Jul Aug Sept Oct Nov Dec
5 15 25
Time of day (LAT)
1klx
10klx
20klx
30klx
40klx
50klx
60klx
Note: All illuminance values in kilolux
Areas shaded indicate illuminance values exceeding 10 klux
All data extracted from BRE publication 'Availability of Daylight,' 1979

Figure 7 Daylight availability.

Typical cross section.

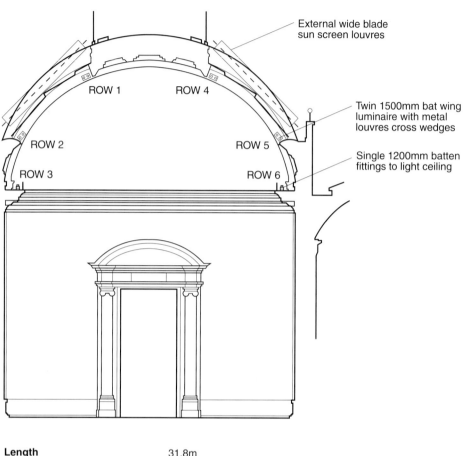

External wide blade sun screen louvres

ROW 1   ROW 4

Twin 1500mm bat wing luminaire with metal louvres cross wedges

ROW 2   ROW 5

Single 1200mm batten fittings to light ceiling

ROW 3   ROW 6

Length	31.8m
Width	9.7m
Height	(max) 11.7m
Floor area	308m^2
Hanging area approx	m^2
Installed loads	26.4 W/m^2 floor area
	15.4 W/m^2 hanging area

Figure 8   Gallery 9, Tate Gallery, London.

Cross section of typical bay

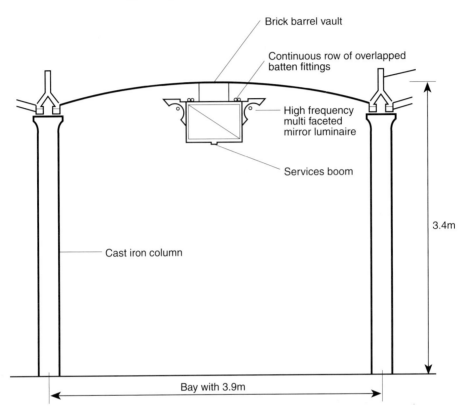

Brick barrel vault

Continuous row of overlapped batten fittings

High frequency multi faceted mirror luminaire

Services boom

Cast iron column

3.4m

Bay with 3.9m

Details of a typical small upper gallery

Length	23.4m
Width	11.7m
Height	(max) 3.4m
Floor area	273m^2
Hanging area approx	200m^2 excluding temporary walls
Installed loads	18.9 W/m^2 floor area excluding tungsten accent lighting 25.8 W/m^2 hanging area

Figure 9 Typical Gallery Tate in the North, Liverpool.

Table 1 Illuminance levels (lux) measured in Gallery 9 (*Figures in brackets relate to uniformity ratio.*)

Height (m) above floor level	Distance along wall from a corner	
	6.25m	12.5m
4.0	280 (1.29)	308 (1.42)
3.5	328 (1.51)	361 (1.67)
3.0	341 (1.57)	376 (1.74)
2.5	337 (1.56)	373 (1.72)
2.0	321 (1.48)	354 (1.63)
1.5	301 (1.39)	333 (1.54)
1.0	277 (1.28)	308 (1.42)
0.5	249 (1.15)	277 (1.28)
0	216 (—)	241 (1.11)

End-wall illumination is good and the overall uniformity from a measuring position at floor level in the corner of the gallery to the peak level on the side walls is better than 1:3. As can be seen from the Table above, the uniformity ratios on side walls are very much better.

The Tate in The North

This gallery[5,6] opened by Prince Charles in 1989, is housed in the fully refurbished and converted warehouse buildings designed by Jesse Hartley in 1840. The buildings occupied by the Tate Gallery form part of the Albert Dock Complex and the massive masonry construction has lent itself to the introduction of energy-efficient air-conditioning which makes use of the large thermal capacity of the building which has largely been retained.

The introduction of air-distribution ductwork and lighting equipment posed a significant problem in that the overall floor to ceiling height in the upper gallery spaces is only 3.4m (see Fig. 9). It was a prime requirement that the original brick barrel vaults should be retained and the introduction of the engineering services was co-ordinated into a services boom housing lighting, electrical cabling, fire-alarm detection and annunciation and public address system.

In addition to severe height restriction there was also the need to light temporary hanging space which could be located on any column line. Each barrel vault therefore had its own services boom so that shadowing created by columns would not be a problem. This meant that lighting fittings had to be located much closer to the hanging zone that would be ideal to achieve the required uniformity ratio of better than 2:1 top to bottom. A number of prototypes and a mock-up led to the adoption of a specially designed low-brightness optic with a reflector with over 20 different facets to focus the light evenly on to the hanging zone. The deep-front louvres give the fitting a very low brightness when viewed obliquely and this was essential to avoid unwanted glare with the low mounting height. Additional lamps were installed on the top side of the boom to provide uplight on the barrel vault which due to the colour cast caused by the red brick were painted white.

The lighting brief required levels on the hanging zone to be variable between 50 and 300 lux and this was achieved by means of high-frequency 1,200mm colour 83 lamps dimmed in groups. The distribution of the control circuits was organised by bay created by the barrel vaults. Typically, an eight-luminaire section of boom running on a notional N-S axis has nine controlled circuits:

  i. Picture lighting: one control circuit for the east side and one for the west.
 ii. 12 volt track, with one circuit on the east side and one on the west.
iii. 12 volt track, with four separate circuits on the bottom of the boom.
 iv. Amenity uplight: one circuit operating both east and west sides of the uplighting on top of the boom.

Overall the installed load is relatively high for a low gallery at 18.9 W/m^2 of floor area, but it must be remembered that typically only the two outer rows of direct illumination would be in use, with possibly some tungsten accent lighting supplementing the uplighters. When the total theoretical maximum hang area is introduced the installed load drops to below 11 W/m^2 of hanging area.

Whitechapel Art Gallery, London

The Whitechapel Art Gallery was built in 1901 and in keeping with galleries of that time makes good use of daylight as the medium to view works of art. Had refurbishment been undertaken in the 1960's, it is probable that the daylight provision would have been omitted. Fortunately, however, refurbishment was not undertaken until the mid 80's and the original daylight provisions were retained with the addition of daylight-linked external small blade blinds. The principle galleries, whilst completely refurbished, retain their original proportions (Figs. 10 and 11) and have been relit using high-frequency 58 watt colour 83 tubes in a recessed and fully integrated fitting which produces a strongly asymmetric output and achieves a very good uniformity ratio down the wall. With the requirement for comparatively small numbers of fittings, and a tight budget, it was necessary to use an off-the-shelf solution and whilst not in their general catalogue, a fitting was available from Philips. This is now marketed as their TCS612.

Cross section of upper gallery

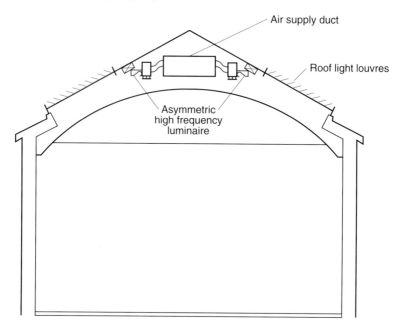

Length	33m
Width	8m
Height	(max) 6m
Floor area	264m²
Hanging area approx	312m²
Installed loads	8.15 W/m² floor area
	6.8 W/m² hanging area

Figure 10 Whitechapel Art Gallery – Upper Gallery.

Set out below are the wall illumination levels (direct light only) that can be expected with this fitting at differing distances from the wall with a 36W lamp in a continuous row.

Cross section of ground floor gallery

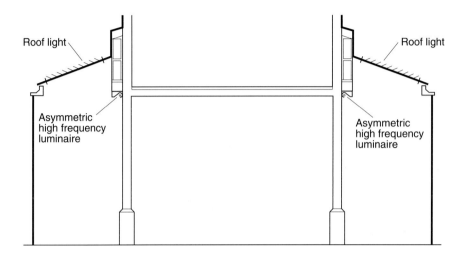

Length	33m
Width	15.4m
Height	5.6m (centre portion)
Floor area	508m^2
Hanging area approx	449m^2
Installed loads	5.8 W/m^2 floor area fluorescent only 6.6 W/m^2 hanging area

Figure 11   Whitechapel Art Gallery – Main Gallery.

Table 2

Distance down wall	Fitting distance from wall					
	0.6m	**0.8m**	**1.0m**	**1.2m**	**1.4m**	**1.6m**
0.5m	1536	1089	828	648	517	420
1.0m	944	954	824	699	589	501
1.5m	400	582	647	624	560	493
2.0m	164	293	402	459	470	449
2.5m	78	148	228	228	340	359
Uniformity Ratio	**19.6**	**7.35**	**3.63**	**2.36**	**1.73**	**1.39**

As can be seen, the uniformity ratio gets progressively worse as the fitting gets closer to the wall with an excessively bright patch near the top. At distances greater than 1.4m from the wall the uniformity ratio is better than 2:1 and in practice, reflected light from the floor, particularly if it is light in colour, assists in lifting the lower wall levels and again improves uniformity.

The installed loads for the galleries are very low at about 8 and 6 W/m² for the upper and lower galleries respectively. Track lighting can be added if necessary to light sculpture or other works in the central areas of the ground-floor gallery, but for normal purposes if there are no works on display in this area, recessed circular fluorescent lamps are used to lift the level generally without distraction from the hangings on the long walls.

Gallery 33, Tate Gallery, London

This is a recently opened new gallery at the Tate Gallery in London, again making good use of daylight. The externally daylight louvres are computer controlled to obscure direct sunlight and thus control UV penetration and excessive exposure to visible light.

Artificial lighting is achieved with a standard asymmetric fitting available from Erco (ref 65486), but with the addition of specially designed louvres to limit longitudinal glare. The fittings are designed for surface mounting, but have been deeply recessed and integrated within the ceiling with the additional louvres flush with the ceiling line.

Each fitting houses twin 36 watt PL lamps (Woton colour 32) and is driven by Philips high-frequency control gear linked to hand-held passive infra red reset devices permitting output to be controlled between 30% and 100%.

Figure 12a shows the arrangement of fittings in the centre of the space and the distances from the end walls requires top-up lighting in these areas. Underrun tungsten halogen lights are used for this purpose and this considerably extends their life and permits better colour matching with the colour 32 lamps.

Cross section

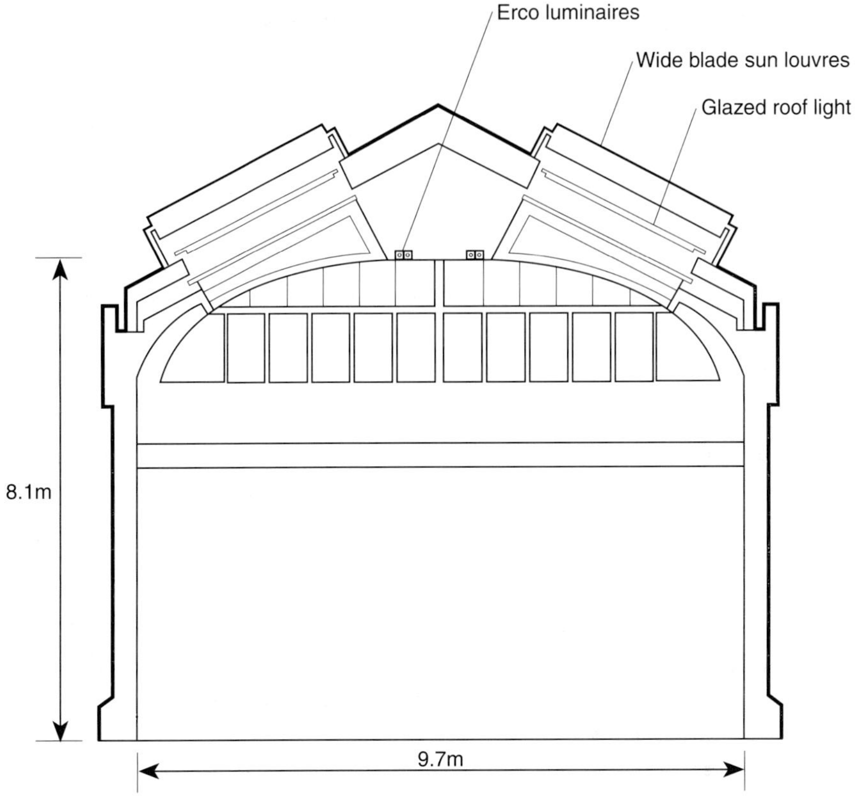

Length		17.5m
Width		9.6m
Height	(max)	8.0m
Floor area		170m²
Hanging area approx		235m²
Installed loads		16.8 W/m² floor area
		13.4 W/m² hanging area

Figure 12   Gallery 33, Tate Gallery, London.

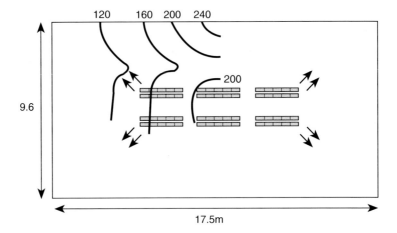

Figure 12a Gallery 33 Plan view showing isolux levels on floor and arrangement of fittings.

Installed loads are in the order of 17 W/m² of the floor area but it would not normally be necessary to use all installed lighting at full level. Indeed the Tate have developed 3 different lighting scenarios, each with much lower power requirements, by presetting the outputs of each row of the fluorescent lighting. Overall running costs are low due to the high level of daylight contribution available.

Check list for energy-efficient lighting design in museums and galleries

    i. Is maximum use of daylight within achieved?

    ii. Is ultraviolet content of daylight adequately controlled?

   iii. Is artificial lighting energy-efficient in terms of lumen output per watt of electrical power?

   iv. Is artificial light used directly or indirectly? Light which is reflected once require 30 or 40% more installed load but with uv absorbing paints it is possible to minimise uv content of the light falling on the exhibit.

    v. Are the exhibits overlit? Could lower levels permit good viewing conditions and reduce overall exposure and energy consumption?

   vi. Is daylight excluded when the gallery is closed to visitors? Exposure with no visitors present is counter-productive and therefore it is normal to minimise illumination levels as far as possible when not required.

  vii. Is artificial light 'off' when the gallery is closed to visitors?

viii. Is artificial lighting 'off' or dimmed when there is adequate daylight?

ix. Do maintenance routines retain the original lighting performance? Are fittings clean, particularly if dimming equipment can be used to compensate for loss of light output?

Conclusion

Whilst tungsten lighting remains an option there are very many other and more energy-efficient sources available to the gallery lighting designer. Recent improvements in colour-rendering properties as well as the opportunities for simple and low-cost dimming permit their use in many circumstances. Whilst initial costs can be, but not always, higher, this is more than offset by lower energy costs and lower maintenance costs, and very much improved reliability.

Acknowledgements

The author is grateful for the assistance of his Partner Dusan Markovic and the members of the SVM lighting team – Hugh McCarthy, Roger Gardner, Bob Locker and Tom Blake.

References

1. Taylor, A. H. and Pracejus, W. G., *Illuminating Engineer*, 45, 1950, p.149.
2. Cady, W. and Appel, W., 'American Dyestuffs', Report 18, 1929, p.407.
3. Mantle, H., 'The Problems of Conservation and Display in Museums Lighting Design', *BSE*, August 1972, pp.99–105.
4. Carver, M., 'The Control of Daylight in the Clore Gallery for Turner Collection' in CIBSE National Lighting Conference, 1988.
5. Boyden, J. and Gardner, R. L., 'Tate Gallery Liverpool', *International Lighting Review* 1/90.
6. McCarthy, H. L. and Gardner, R. L., The Liverpool View in CIBSE National Lighting Conference, 1988.

Biography

Michael Carver is a Director/Partner with The Steensen Varming Mulcahy Partnership, a leading firm of consulting engineers specialising in all forms of environmental control within buildings. The Practice has for many years been involved in specialist lighting design for museums and galleries and is currently retained by the Trustees of the Tate Gallery, the Soane Museum and the Trustees of the Henry Moore Foundation. Michael Carver became an Associate Partner in 1981 and an Equity Partner in 1986. In that time he has been involved in the engineering design of many buildings paying particular attention to energy efficiency. He was very much involved with the design and development of the control systems for daylight and artificial light within the new Clore Gallery for the Turner Collection.

Environmental Improvements and Energy Efficiency in Whitby Museum

David Pybus The Whitby Museum, North Yorkshire
John Wm Morris Yorkshire and Humberside Museums Council

Introduction

This paper sets out the steps taken by The Whitby Literary and Philosophical Society to improve the environment in their museum. It was also considered appropriate to examine the energy used by the museum and to make any possible reductions. Due to limited funding, proposals have to be self-financing in the short term, or should demonstrate that the cost benefit will be such that any capital expenditure will be recovered within five years.

History

By the early 19th century, societies devoted to learning and philosophy were springing up in many northern towns. In each case, one declared purpose was the establishment of a museum to house curiosities of nature and objects of antiquity. Whitby did not lag behind. On 28th November 1822, a circular letter went to selected residents: 'For some time past a number of Gentlemen in Whitby have wished to have a Society formed for collecting and supporting a Whitby Museum'. The response was favourable and Whitby Literary and Philosophical Society was formed on 17th January 1823 and continues to the present day. By September 1823, there was sufficient material to display before the public in 'two commodious' rooms rented for the purpose in Baxtergate. On the 3rd January 1827, a new museum was formally opened on the top floor of the new 'Whitby Public Baths, Library and Museum', a building erected especially for the purpose. By 1857, the Society had bought the whole building which served as the museum for the next seventy-four years.

Several attempts at expansion produced no suitable premises. A possible site did however exist to the rear of the Art Gallery, built in 1925, to house the painting collection of the late Alderman Pannett. The Trustees of the Estate agreed to allow the Society to build an extension, and on 5th August 1931 the present museum (Fig. 1) was officially opened.

Figure 1 Whitby Museum from the north east.
Photograph by David Pybus.

Collections

The museum's collections reflect the approach of a long-established Philosophical Society. They are extremely varied and contain geology, archaeology, industrial archaeology (including shipping, alum and jet-mining), ethnography, fauna and flora and social history. The Whitby area is particularly rich in palaeontology and the collection contains saurian material, type and figured ammonites and belemnites. From the academic viewpoint this forms one of the oldest and most important elements of the museum.

There is, however, an added dimension which reflects the activities and acquisitions of the Whitby seafarers. Whitby was an important port in the 17th, 18th and 19th centuries. Vessels, whether whaling in the Arctic, exploring in the Pacific or trading all over the world, returned to their home port with curios for the museum. This has resulted in collections of major significance – particularly on ethnography and whaling. Whitby was the home port of James Cook, and the museum contains both archive and objects relating to him and his pioneering Pacific voyages. William Scoresby Junior was not only a whaler like his father, but carried out early scientific work on electricity and magnetism and corresponded with Michael Faraday. The importance of the Scoresby Collection is only now being recognised.

However, after the initial effort in the 1820's to assemble a collection, particularly of local fossils, material was added without a defined collection policy. The stimulus of a spacious new building in 1931 has resulted in the acquisition of numerous artifacts and a shortage of space ever since.

The museum building

The Society leases the building for a peppercorn rent from Whitby Town Council who are the residual beneficiaries of the site following a series of local government re-organisations. The Town Council is responsible for the cost of building maintenance, heating, lighting and caretakers' salaries. The outgoings are financed by a proportion of the admission charges and by support from a precept added to the Council Tax. Currently there is an operational cost of £8,000 per annum, financed by the Council. The museum is open for fifty-one hours per week during the twenty-two week summer period, and for twenty-nine hours per week for the thirty-week winter period.

On plan the building approximates to a square which has had four minor extensions constructed at the corners (Fig. 2). The building is mainly single storey with a partial basement and limited mezzanine floors to two areas. The total floor area is 1,086 sq.m (11,300 sq.ft) of which 840 sq.m (8,750 sq.ft), just over 77%, are devoted to display galleries. The building was constructed with cavity walled brickwork and a flat concrete roof. Subsequently, the roof failed and a new pitched roof was constructed in 1986 over the existing roof.

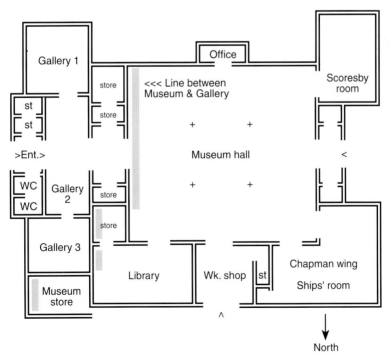

Figure 2   Ground Floor Plan of Whitby Museum and Art Gallery. (Not to scale.)

At present there are several major faults with the structure, including failure of the wall ties between the leaves of brick in the cavity walls, persistent water penetration of the basement areas, and a general deterioration of the heating plant. A recent survey undertaken by the Borough Council identified approximately £100,000 of essential repair work needed to bring the fabric into good condition. Neither the Town nor Borough Council is prepared or able to fund this work.

In addition to the deteriorating fabric, there was a need to improve the environment within the museum to meet acceptable standards. Illumination levels were generally too high – in some areas, very high – with variable heating and relative humidity levels. Both problems needed addressing, but with the limited funding available, it was obvious that consideration had to be given to revenue expenditure as well as capital funding. The first named author of this paper is the museum's Honorary Curator of Archaeology who is employed as the Chief Chemist & Energy Manager for a major potash mine and refinery. With this expertise available, the museum was able to make a sound financial case for examining the cost-savings which could result from energy efficiency, and at the same time improve environmental conditions for the Collections.

Surveys
Fabric

During 1991, the building had been the subject of a structural survey commissioned by Scarborough Borough Council as part of a review of their building stock. This listed the various defects and indicated that they were leading to a damaging indoor environment and excessive waste of energy.

Environmental conditions survey

The environmental data referred to in this paper covers the period from the 14th of June 1991 to the 17th of January 1992. Three recording thermohygrographs were used in various locations, both within the Galleries and inside certain showcases. The positions were noted using the 'object location format' (Fig. 3), a system which records the position of objects throughout the museum. By reference to a plan of the building, it becomes possible to pinpoint a zone, an area and a location where monitoring is taking place.

The thermohygrographs were calibrated at the start of recording. At the end of the period there was a further check to establish whether inaccuracies had developed. There was no significant error in temperature readings, but the three thermohygrographs all recorded higher relative humidity readings, ranging from 2% to 4%. Further recordings are proposed to assist in the design for the new central heating-plant.

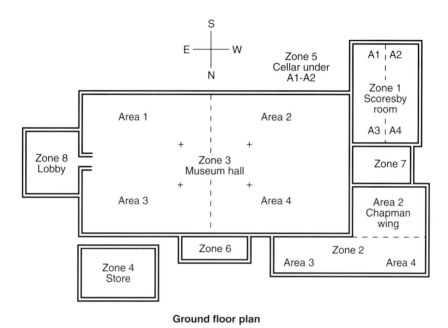

Ground floor plan

Figure 3 Object location format.

The recordings confirmed many of the assumed conditions and also indicated conditions which were not known. The influence of solar gain through the walls was more than had been expected and indicates that additional insulation is needed. The temperature gradients, both vertically and horizontally within the display areas, are more extreme than previously thought and point to the need for mechanically assisted air movement. A sample of the data obtained during the survey is set out in Tables 1a and 1b.

Table 1a % Relative Humidity – Weekly Range.

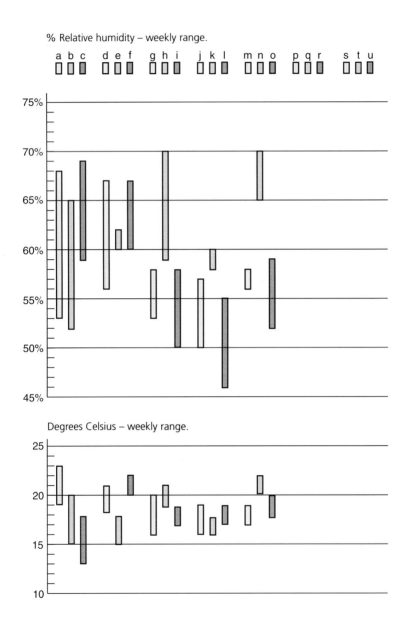

Table 1b Position of Thermohygrograph Recorders on the Object Location Plan, Date of Observation and Reference to Graphs in **Table 1a**.

Zone	Location	Date	Graph	Comment
1	A4/W.Wall	120791	(a)	Large variation: solar gain on West Wall.
1	A2/W.Wall	081191	(b)	Indication of damp penetration from *cellar.
1	A2/W.Wall	081191	(c)	Inside globe case same location as (b).
1	A1/C66 O/S C66	011191	(d)	Short period of daily use of heating causing instability.
1	A1/C66	011191	(e)	Away from the West Wall the conditions improve, the case assists stability.
2	A4/W.Wall	190791	(f)	Instability due to solar heating on West Wall.
2	A3 inside Case C26	251091	(g)	Short drops in RH due to central heating.
3	A1 S.Wall	120791	(h)	Stable temperature, trace shows rapid change in RH possibly due to effect of climatic changes caused by front door.
3	A1/C8 Outside	061291	(i)	Regular variation in temperature and humidity following central heating time clock.
3	A2/C58 O/S Case	291191	(j)	The temperature curve indicates proximity to a heating source.
3	A2/C58 I/S Case	291191	(k)	The temperature curve is flattened with a satisfactory RH value and stability.
3	A3/C56 O/S Case	061291	(l)	Case 56 is not as well sealed as Case 58 which shows in the RH curve.
3	A3/C56 I/S Case	061291	(m)	The case is providing some buffering against a steady reduction of RH in the room.
3	A4 Pillar 4	020891	(n)	High humidity probably due to free interchange through open front door.
3	A4/C22 Outside	291191	(o)	Humidity level approximates to 55% RH for a mean temperature of 19°.

Energy use

Initial examination showed that there was room for extensive savings if more effective energy management could be introduced. There are

obvious problems with the shared use of the building between the Art
Gallery, administered by Whitby Town Council, and the area occupied by
the Society's Museum. The setting up of a joint management committee to
examine the problems of the building as a whole has led to closer
collaboration between the two.

The first task was a survey of the existing electrical installation. It was
relatively simple to count the light bulbs and with four electricity meters in
the entrance, the task of reconciling consumption with occupancy should
have been simple. Unfortunately, this was not the case.

The building is located on the top of a hill in a relatively exposed
position surrounded by Pannett Park. Within the park is an aviary, and the
gardeners' store and mess-room is situated in the basement of the main
building. The meters were unlabelled apart from one marked 'Aviary &
Gardeners' Store'. The Town Council was able to supply the bills paid for
gas, water and electricity over a number of years. It appeared that two
meters served the museum and one meter the Art Gallery, and were the
responsibility of Whitby Town Council. A separate meter recorded consumption by the Aviary and gardeners' toilet and was the responsibility of
Scarborough Borough Council.

In order to sort out which meter was recording what, professional
help was sought. Cleveland Potash supplied a trainee electrical engineer
and an electrical apprentice who traced the power and lighting circuits
back to the meters and produced system drawings of the actual installation. Recommendations were made to ensure future modifications were
safe and rational.

As a result of this survey, it was discovered that the Borough Council
gardeners' mess-room's supply of electricity was taken from the museum
office's distribution board and recorded by a private meter, which used to
be read, but whose very existence had been forgotten. This anomaly
caused some confusion: the Town Council clerk was unaware of the meter
and Scarborough Borough Council had not been charged for the electricity for six years. Attempts to identify retrospectively the gardeners'
consumption proved futile as the meter was faulty and reading backwards
at a variable rate. No further effort has been made to quantify this
consumption and Scarborough Borough Council will in future be
invoiced for consumption registered on a new replacement meter.

Improvements
Lighting system

The first saving was achieved by Northern Electric helpfully billing all
three museum meters to one account – thus eliminating the cost of two

standing charges. This was possible because each phase of a three-phase supply was individually metered and adjacent to each other.

Advantage was taken of the opportunity to analyse the data from previous gas and electricity accounts with XSDetect, a monitoring and targeting computer programme based around Lotus 123 and supplied by Vilnis Vesma Ltd. It is used at Cleveland Potash Ltd for their complex monitoring and targeting requirements. It allows the easy entry of data, and performs some date arithmetic, which smooths out variations between the bills and different time periods allowing a rational analysis to be performed.

By attempting to link calculations of specific consumptions to poss-ible influencing factors, it was demonstrated very clearly that there was no relationship between energy costs and any parameter of demand; for example, occupancy, opening hours, weather conditions. The programme allowed a base load for gas and electricity consumption to be determined. This load was used as a standard against which the extent of energy waste could be identified. It became possible to identify various ways of achiev-ing savings. Because it has proved so useful, the museum intends to continue monitoring energy use with this software and to develop the system to include all measurable parameters related to the running of the museum. The programme also identified historic energy changes which had been made (Table 2), some unintentional, as a result of the new roof which eliminated the use of natural light which had been possible through the original roof, leaks in the heating pipework and by restricted use of the lights in the side galleries of the Art Gallery. This last measure was an emergency cost-saving introduced by Whitby Town Council which required that these particular pictures should be lit only on demand.

Table 2 Quarterly electrical consumption for the years 1985, 1986, 1991 and 1993 assuming a 40% saving in consumption due to re-lamping.

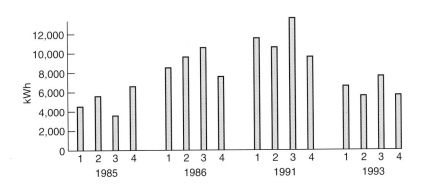

Note:
1. The large increase in consumption between 1985 and 1986 (181%) was due to the new roof construction. Up to this time, the main gallery had natural light entering through roof lights.
2. There is a steady increase in consumption between 1986 and 1991 due to additional appliances being added.

The present electrical installation dates from 1976. The original specification was soon superceded by 'improvements': another fitting here, another spot-light there. The galleries were lit using spot-lights mounted on a track system. Creeping expansion was therefore a simple matter of clipping in the fitting. Unfortunately each of the spot-lights was rated at 150 watts and there was a total of 116 in the Museum and Art Gallery. With occupancy of approximately 1992 hours per year, the energy bill for the spot-lights alone amounted to £3,143.7 per annum.

The prospect of changing the existing track was not considered economic on grounds of cost and disturbance. Thorn Lighting, the manufacturer of the original track system, was approached for suggestions. It was pointed out that the cheapest and easiest way of replacing the lights was to retain the existing track system and Edison screw lampholders. Replacement units were available for the existing PAR 38 light bulbs, which were simply removed. The replacement units were Thorn TQEP 35 fittings. Each of these consists of an electronic transformer, contained within the rear housing, which provides a 12V supply to a 35W low-voltage quartz halogen bulb. The fittings allow for dichroic reflectors, UV.filters, or coloured filters if necessary.

These units are individually expensive, but a critical examination of lighting requirements and illuminance levels indicated that the number of fittings could be reduced from 116 to approximately 80. Thorn Lighting generously provided the fittings at a discount in return for potential publicity. The energy saved by this proposal was calculated on 1992 hours of use per year and a comparison between the original and replacement lamps and fittings is seen in Table 3.

Table 3 Energy-saving due to replacement of PAR 38 light fittings by Thorn TQEP 35 low voltage quartz halogen fittings.

Lamp Type	No. of Lamps	Wattage	Total Wattage	Cost per Kw/hr	Total Cost	Annual Cost
PAR 38	116	150	17.4 kW	9.07p.	£1.58	£3143.7
Low V. Quartz Halogen	80	35	2.8 kW	9.07p.	£0.25	£ 505.9

With electricity currently at 9.07 pence per unit and occupancy of 1992 hours per year, this means a saving of £2,638 per annum. Comparing average opening hours with the expected life of the new lamps, an annual replacement cost in the order of £240 per year is expected, which leaves a nett saving in the order of £2,398 per year. The previous replacement cost of the PAR 38 lamps was not recorded as a specific item, but must have approximated to the projected annual replacement cost of the lamps in the new units. A PAR 38 bulb has an expected life of 1,500 hours at a cost of £5.85 plus VAT, compared with the bulb life of 3,500 hours for a Lightstream dichroic lamp at a cost of £7.71 plus VAT (June 1992), which is supplied with the TQEP 35 fitting.

This work has now been implemented at a cost of £2,300. The first indication is that electricity consumption has been reduced by 41%. This should save 19,123 kW/hrs per year resulting in a saving of approximately £1,734 in the first year. Further savings are possible as the above calculation assumes that all the lamps are on during opening hours. In the winter months, there are very few visitors, and consideration has been given to using passive infrared detectors to switch on the lamps in response to visitor presence. The economic case for this proposal is much harder to make following the introduction of low wattage lamps. However, there is a dual benefit, a further reduction in cost of approximately £250 per annum and a reduction in illuminance exposure of the collection, a sound passive conservation measure. A further proposal under consideration will examine the introduction of down lighters to give sufficient light for circulation and cleaning purposes so that the main lighting system is switched on only during opening hours.

Heating system

A survey of the condition and layout of the heating system was carried out. The existing heating system comprises a gas-fired boiler rated at 234.5kW (800,000 Btu/hr) supplying three ring-main piping systems located in ducts with floor grills. In the later extensions, these pipes surface to supply radiators, some of which are fitted with thermostatic valves. The only other control of heating is a water circulation thermostat to protect the boiler and a time-switch.

The manufacturer (Beeston) confirmed that the boiler is at or near the end of its useful life with the prospect of increasingly regular and expensive repairs over the years. The possibility always existed that the next failure would be the last, due to lack of spare parts.

A Satchwell climatronic weather compensator and motorised valve had been installed originally, but according to a note scrawled on a piece of cardboard it had been disconnected by someone at some time in the past, and for some unknown reason!

The heating system is switched off during the summer months according to standard local authority practice. An analysis of the gas bills for the boiler indicated that during the heating season, the boiler is on, whether it is needed or not. There is no relationship between gas consumption and occupancy hours or degree days (an indication of heating requirements). The gas bills were examined and the following information was extracted.

Table 4 Quarterly gas consumption for the years 1985, 1986, 1991.

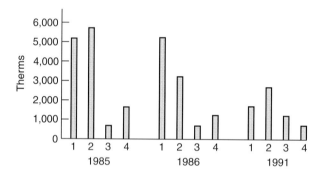

The marked decline in gas consumption between 1985 and 1986 was the result of the construction of a new pitched roof and the associated insulation. Gas consumption dropped from 12,327 Therms to 9,234 Therms, a reduction of 25%. This saving was gained at the expense of additional electrical energy used for extra lighting, equivalent to 546 Therms (see the note below Table 2). Further reduction during 1991 is not due to any intentional saving, but indicates that the whole system is deteriorating to the extent that sections of the pipe runs are no longer useable and are closed down. The use of the building has remained constant throughout the period, without complaints from the occupants. It is therefore possible that the previous level of heating was excessive.

The survey detected marked changes of temperature in adjacent galleries and considerable temperature variation between floor and ceiling.

Certain modifications have been considered in order to increase flexibility and to match the boiler output to the heating requirement. One scheme proposed that two boilers be fitted: a condensing boiler operating continuously at maximum efficiency to take the base load, and a dual firing position conventional boiler to provide incremental heat additions according to demand. A second scheme proposed the use of up to four large domestic boilers with the necessary control equipment to allow for differing loads. Consideration has also been given to partial control of humidity within the galleries by varying ambient temperature, or by maintaining a constant temperature, and controlling the humidity by other means.

The gradual decline of the heating plant came to a head when a large section of the circulation pipework failed. Due to inaccessible ducts, it will now be necessary to re-route flow and return pipes through the galleries. Random heat-loss from exposed pipes is likely to produce 'hot spots' and make it very difficult to maintain an even temperature in the galleries. All pipe-runs will have to be insulated to avoid casual heat loss and individual thermostatic radiator valves may be necessary. These changes are still being considered and plans for alterations to the heating system have not yet been finalised.

Water

A third consumable product is purchased, namely water. Although a minor cost within the whole expenditure on services, nevertheless water costs showed potential for economies. The standing-charges in particular constitute a major component of the annual cost, but with a urinal cistern operating continuously, there was considerable scope for savings. If the cistern is discharged only during opening hours, a rough estimate of the saving on water and sewage costs alone is:

Table 5 Reduction in sewage cost.

Duration of Consumption	Nos of Hours	Cubic m. per Year	Cost per Unit	Annual Cost
Continuous running system	8760 hrs	160 (actual)	£1.47 per cubic m.	£219
Running during opening hours	1992 hrs	37 (estimated)	£1.47 per cubic m.	£ 50

Table 5 does not include the standing charges of £22.5 for water and £61.5 for sewerage. Yorkshire Water charges 45 pence per cubic metre for water with a sewerage charge based on 95% of consumption of 92 pence per cubic metre.

Solutions

Matters relating to the improvement of the museum fabric are delegated to the Development Sub-Committee of the Society. This Committee considered various methods of supporting Whitby Town Council with the implementation of energy-saving measures. A short presentation was made to the Executive Committee of the Town Council at which all the energy-costs and potential savings were demonstrated. It was suggested that, for a period of five years, the Society should act as agents for the management of gas, electric, water and sewage services. During this time the Whitby Town Council would make a regular payment to the Society in respect of energy-costs. This fixed monthly payment was set below the present energy-costs in anticipation of the predicted savings. The Society would take responsibility for paying the energy bills and making any investments necessary to reduce running costs from its building fund. This proposal was formally approved by both parties and is now in effect.

The benefits to the Council are that:
   i. They have a fixed outlay for 5 years.
  ii. They do not have to make the initial investments required to reduce the energy costs, i.e. the capital cost of the new boiler installation.
 iii. At the end of the term of the agreement, the Council resumes responsibility for what will then be lower payments for energy.

The benefits to the Society are that:
   i. The improvements to the museum climate can be made quickly.
  ii. The Society is able to seek sponsorship towards some or all of the work from sources not available to the Council.
 iii. By helping the Council to reduce their energy costs, more funds become available for maintenance of the fabric.
  iv. There are associated publicity opportunities.

The Regional Officer from the Energy Efficiency Office of the Department of Energy was notified of this project out of courtesy. As museums are not a targeted sector, the Department of Energy is unable to provide anything more than moral support at the moment. A peripatetic Energy Adviser is available who can help, provide advice and make suggestions. The Energy Management Assistance Scheme, introduced in 1992, could provide financial support for energy consultancy but not installation costs.

Future improvements

In addition to the proposed heating installation and the modifications to the lighting fittings, the following energy-saving measures are being considered.

1.   The cavities of the external brick walls could be filled with blown-fibre insulation.

2. The windows, particularly on the south and west elevations, could be double-glazed and shaded.
3. The front doors could be improved by fitting a draught lobby to prevent surges of external air entering the building.
4. The warm air near the ceiling in the galleries could be re-distributed to make better use of available heat.
5. The small individual electrical water heaters could be replaced by a domestic supply drawn from a calorifier situated on the primary flow and return.
6. The electricity tariff could be changed to a 'maximum demand tariff'.

Policy

Within independent, volunteer-run museums, there can be a steady change of personalities and therefore the necessity to record definite policy statements is crucial. For this reason, a formal energy policy was written. It was agreed that a person should be nominated to act as an Energy Manager, whose defined activities include:

   i. operating the museum in the most energy-efficient manner within the constraints of collection care.
   ii. responsibility for monitoring the energy efficiency of the heating and lighting systems and for proposing improvements as necessary.
   iii. increasing awareness of energy efficiency amongst employees and volunteers.
   iv. holding regular quarterly reviews of performance.
   v. monitoring the museum environment and comparing this with desirable performance levels.
   vi. preparing reports for submission to the appropriate Committees.

Conclusion

Energy-costs are the second largest bill after wages at the museum. Energy-waste is not immediately obvious as most people are not exposed to the consequences of their usage. In these days of financial constraints, there are tremendous cost-savings which can be made whilst at the same time improving the museum environment and reducing the need for future treatment of objects damaged due to variations in ambient temperature and humidity.

It should not be forgotten that there is a tremendous amount of assistance and advice freely available, and that small museums enjoy considerable goodwill both within their own community and from statutory bodies. The benefit to the museum of this assistance and advice has been invaluable and the Committee and Members of the Society would like to express their gratitude to all concerned. Whitby Museum was in the first group of independent museums to obtain Registration in the Yorkshire and Humberside Museums Council area under the Museum & Galleries Commission's Registration Scheme. With the second stage of this scheme, likely to include forward-planning in all areas of museum activities, museums should start to consider environmental control and energy-management issues now.

Acknowledgements

The Society would like to thank the following for their help and involvement: BRECSU for technical advice and support; British Gas for the design of the proposed Heating System; Cleveland Potash Ltd for support in the preparation of the electrical survey by providing a trainee engineer and apprentice; Rodol Ltd for the supply of water treatment chemicals; Vilnis Vesma for a licence to develop a museum application of his software and Yorkshire and Humberside Museums Council for help, advice and support.

References

Energy Efficiency Office, *Introduction to Energy Efficiency in Museums, Galleries, Libraries and Churches*, 1994.

Energy Efficiency Office, *Fuel Efficiency Booklets*: Energy Audits, no.1; Degree Days, no.7; The Economic Thickness of Insulation for Hot Water Pipes, no.8; Economic Use of Electricity, no.9; Controls and Energy Saving, no.10; Energy Management and Good Lighting Practice, no.12; Economic Use of Gas-fired Boiler Plant, no.15; Economic Thickness of Insulation for Existing Industrial Buildings, no.16, 1990.

Energy Efficiency Office, *Good Practice Guide*: Computer Aided Monitoring and Targeting for Industry, no.31, 1991.

Useful addresses

Building Research Energy Conservation Support Unit (BRECSU)
Building Research Establishment
Garston
Watford
Hertfordshire, WD2 7JR
Tel. No. 0923 664258

Energy Efficiency Office,
Department of Environment,
Blackhorse Road,
London, SE8 5JH

Vilnis Vesma
17, Church Street
Newent
Gloucestershire, GL18 1PU
Tel. No. 0531 821350
Fax. No. 0531 820603

Biographies

David Pybus was born in Sandsend near Whitby and has lived in one of the two places for almost all his life. He has been employed at Cleveland Potash Ltd in the Analytical Laboratory since 1973, and in 1978 he was appointed Senior Analyst and Chief Chemist in 1987. Subsequently he was given additional responsibility of Energy Manager in 1990. Cleveland Potash's Boulby Mine site, located near Whitby, uses energy in the form of electricity and fuel oil, accounting for £6.5m per annum or approximately 14.5% of the company's costs. He was invited to be Honorary Archaeological Curator at Whitby Museum and member of the Management Committee and Development Sub-Committee.

John Wm. Morris worked initially in the field of Architectural Conservation and is now Assistant Director (Technical) at Yorkshire and Humberside Museums Council. For the past twenty-one years, he has been involved closely with technical support for fine-art and museum collections. Part of his function is to advise members of the Museums Council on monitoring, and, where necessary, correcting adverse environmental conditions.

David Pybus and John Morris are both members of the Whitby Literary and Philosophical Society.

The National Museum of Photography, Film and Television, Bradford:

An Exercise in Environmental Control, Energy Efficiency and Financial Savings

Tim Whitehouse Formerly National Museum of Photography, Film and Television, Bradford

Introduction

The City of Bradford Metropolitan Council had, since 1963, a vast six-storey building in the city centre which had remained empty since its construction. The National Museum of Science and Industry had extensive collections of photography, film and television, and before 1983 had insufficient space in which to display them. After long discussions and consultation between the Science Museum and Bradford Council, the National Museum of Photography, Film and Television (NMPFT) was founded in Bradford, West Yorkshire, in 1983. The brave decision by a national museum to open a second northern outpost was instrumental in the resurgence which established Bradford as a tourist attraction and an economically rejuvenated city.

Figure 1 Exterior of the National Museum of Photography, Film and Television.

The building's construction as a theatre ideally suited the IMAX film format and the centre of the building houses Britain's only IMAX auditorium, with a screen measuring some 19.5m x 16m. Nineteen major galleries house the history and science of photography, film and television and major collections include the entire Kodak Museum which was moved from Harrow in 1984 and opened in Bradford in 1989, and The Daily Herald Archive, comprising almost 1.3 million photographs and over 100,000 glass negatives. The museum's policy is to show to its visitors the art as well as the technology of these media and its special exhibition galleries were partly financed by the Arts Council of Great Britain's 'Housing the Arts' Fund. With two cinemas, and work progressing to open a library of significant and representative television programmes in 1993–94, the museum's coverage of the three media continues to grow.

To ensure the collection is maintained and displayed in the most appropriate climate, strict guidelines for environmental conditions are set by the Collections Management Group, which comprises a registrar, two curators, an information officer and a security adviser. In a museum with such varied collections, environmental conditions will always have to be a compromise among the needs of different types of materials, ranging from wood, leather and paper to metal and glass. Thus the environment needs adjustment in the light of the condition of these materials. Temperature and relative humidity are the same for both display and storage spaces where 18.5°C ± 1.5°C and 47.5%RH ± 5% is the target. Storage/archive spaces are lit when required to a maximum 150 lux and a maximum of 25µW/lumen of ultraviolet radiation. Displays are lit to a maximum of 150 lux and 40 µW/lumen.

History of mechanical and electrical services

The mechanical and electrical services were mostly installed at the time of the building's construction in 1963, and the museum therefore has a considerable amount of equipment which is over twenty-years old, but which in many cases has only seen eight years' service. The main gallery air-handling unit was not designed to supply conditioned air suitable for museum objects. Its design specification was to provide ventilation with comfort cooling for people, and no humidification or dehumidification. The conversion to a museum saw the installation of a Vapac Steam Humidifier which did little to improve conditions, but which convinced a few people that the museum was now air-conditioned! In total there are seven separate air-conditioning systems serving the IMAX auditorium, the IMAX projection box, the Multi Media projection box, the Kodak Museum, the main galleries, the television galleries and the Pictureville Cinema.

Three 293 kW Allen Ygnis boilers provided low-temperature hot water; a four-stage Reacis Chiller (only two stages worked correctly when the museum took the building over) provided chilled water; various heat-rejection condensers were roof-mounted, and each gallery had eight fan-coil units with heating and cooling coils each with integral electro-mechanical thermostats, which were proving extremely unreliable and difficult to calibrate. Hot water was provided by two giant horizontal calorifiers fed off the central boiler circuit. Kodak plant was all electric consisting of a 36 kW electric boiler, point-of-use electric domestic hot water, a Daikin chiller and electric-heater batteries in the Flakt air-handling unit.

The mainly Satchwell and Honeywell controls were not calibrated correctly and in many cases the detectors were not located in the correct position for the function they were trying to perform. The control strategy did not make use of free cooling or have the ability to attempt de-humidification. The settings were often at variance to those of the gallery fan coils and in most cases the low-limit supply temperature set point was set too high to cool the galleries to anywhere near the required tempera-ture in summer. Maintenance had been seriously neglected to the point that, once an in-depth analysis of the plant and its log books had been carried out, it proved necessary to set up and commission the plant from scratch.

This combined to make the environmental conditions in the museum the subject of many discussions between the curatorial teams and the Property Services Agency, which had responsibility for the building prior to 1988.

Thermohydrograph readings from that period show typical relative humidity and temperature ranges of as much as ±20%RH and ±6°C respectively. Consequently, the museum had dissatisfied curatorial staff, out-of-date, poorly maintained and inadequate services and no energy-efficiency programme. Thus the challenge was set!

The indoor environment

Who makes decisions on environmental control and on what basis are they made?

The museum has its own climatology team, which in effect consists of a curator/interpreter and the Estates Manager, who meet frequently to assess the environment and set conditions.

This structure works quite well, as it is unrestricted by normal constraints of committees and it is small enough to ensure personal accountability.

Since the museum is relatively young, there has not been sufficient time to assess whether the previously discussed central band of 18.5°C and 45% RH represents the best mean conditions to store and display the range of objects in the collection. While the collections appear stable within these conditions, the empirical research programme has still a long way to go and until then the museum will rely on existing printed guidelines, such as Thomson's 'The Museum Environment' to set the parameters for the environmental conditions. Ultimately, the museum hopes its research and expertise will contribute towards defining the standards for environmental conditions necessary for storage and display of collections of photography, film and television.

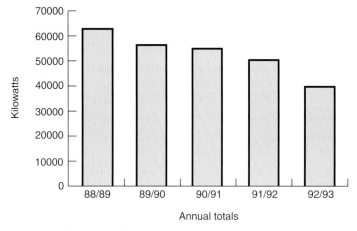

Figure 2 Electricity consumption.

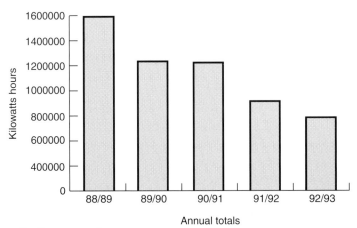

Figure 3 Gas consumption.

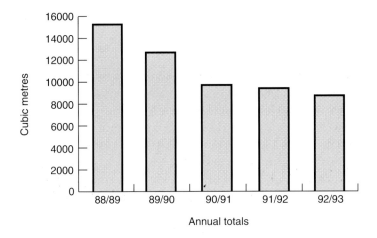

Figure 4 Water consumption.

A major goal is to work within realisable targets for mechanical and electrical services and environmental conditions, as over-ambitious targets would only result in demoralisation amongst staff and ultimately an absence of belief in our goals.

Description of energy targets

The other benefit arising from the link between the curatorial department and the Estates department is to agree a common approach to plant renovations. Until curatorial input became routine, the engineer was assessing the repairs only two-dimensionally; that is, the extent of dilapidation and inefficiency, and the cost of repairs. Curatorial involvement introduced the third dimension, namely the needs of the collection.

The requirements of the collection set the guidelines for assessing improvements. Next came the task of funding and persuading the museum's senior management of the urgency of the work. This was quickly accomplished as management was already aware of the inherent climatic problems.

Funding was not immediately available other than the block allocation from the revenue budget to cover everything from utility costs and maintenance to cleaning. Funding the first stage of renovation of the system therefore had to be found from existing budgets. By mutual agreement, Stage One consisted of improving the controls to the main gallery air-handling unit which was incapable of providing de-humidification, free cooling or motorizing dampers to recirculate good-quality air. The initial cost of approximately £15,000 included the purchase of a Satchwell Building Energy Management System and proved so successful that the entire energy conservation and plant improvement programme can be traced back to this initial work. Whilst all the major works to plant and services were either on the drawing board or had started, an in-depth analysis of utility usage and costs resulting in tariff reductions to both gas and electricity costs were underway. The energy charts on display in the Estates Management Office have become a point of interest amongst staff and make monitoring of alterations/ improvements possible, as well as giving immediate indication of a problem should the line on a graph show an upward movement.

Maintenance procedures were tightened to ensure that any fault contributing to energy wastage was made a priority repair. It had to be carried out within three hours. Tungsten lamps on stairs and other non-display areas were changed during maintenance visits to compact fluorescents, creating a saving of electricity, labour and replacement lamp costs. The installation of 250 lamps costing approximately £3,000, saves the museum in the region of £7,500 per annum.

The museum's internal Newsletter alerted staff of ways to be more energy-conscious and they were made aware, at regular intervals, of progress. The effect was dramatic during the first few weeks following the Newsletter's publication – radiator valves which had not been used for years suddenly came into use before windows were opened.

Senior management saw a financial return on this investment. Staff found conditions improving and money became available for other projects. All who previously thought energy conservation was turning off or turning down started to become inquisitive! The way was now clear for a full assault on energy costs and plant improvement.

Energy-conservation measures

An in-depth survey of mechanical and electrical installations highlighted the problems and resulted in a five-year rectification plan. At first, every scheme was required to:

    i. provide improved climatic conditions.
    ii. provide a return on investment (payback) of less than 1.5 years.
    iii. bring into correct operation previously unsatisfactory plant.
    iv. improve conditions relating to Health and Safety – particularly concerning the bacteria *Legionella pneumophilia*.

Subsequently schemes were installed which simply provided a payback, which by year four had moved to two years instead of 1.5 years. In every case BATNEEC (best available technology not entailing excessive costs) played a central role. Rather surprisingly, approximately 10% of savings were achieved at no cost. Simple alterations to valves supplying automatic flushing urinal cisterns and reducing flushing to twenty-minute intervals instead of every five minutes, provided investment-free savings, as did the rather more theoretically complex but practically simple modification to air-distribution patterns in the main galleries.

Common practice in the air-conditioning industry is to prevent the supply air temperature from falling below 14°C in order to eliminate draughts, which is good in theory. In practice, however, it means that often incoming fresh air is heated at the main air-handling unit only to be cooled by the gallery fan coils to cope with the massive heat gains within each gallery, while still not achieving the desired temperature of 18.5°C.

Each gallery was generating between 8 and 14 kW of sensible heat from lighting and unknown quantities of both latent and sensible heat from occupants.

The latter was outside the museum's control, but by simply adjusting the diffusion pattern of incoming air at the high-level grills to blow the air across the lighting tracks, thus using their heat, the low-limit set point could be removed, thereby eliminating the original wasteful heating and cooling cycle and also increasing lamp life due to cooler operation.

Other very simple schemes, with an almost immediate payback, included the installation of fluorescent lamps with their own independent circuit in each gallery, consuming in total 1.5 kW per gallery. These became known as 'cleaning lights' and they saved at least 100 kW a day or £3,000 a year. They also had the effect of reducing the cooling requirements of the building and the exposure of objects to light. Linked into this, in preparation for the Building Energy Management System (BEMS), each gallery circuit was controlled by a time-clock, thereby eliminating unnecessary wastage.

More major schemes included the removal of the vast DHW storage calorifiers and replacing them with two direct fired gas units, the total cost being in the order of £6,000. Summer gas bills plummeted from an average of £500 a month for the four summer months to under £50 a month. The gas board even sent a team of inspectors round to check whether an illegal device had been fitted to the meter!

The all-electric Kodak plant was converted to gas for a total cost of approximately £10,000, thereby immediately removing 60 kW from the museum's electrical consumption. The payback on this scheme is under one year as the cost for electricity per kW is 6.03 pence against 1.4 pence for a kW of gas. The gallery is now served by two 18 kW condensing boilers, which provide heat and DHW to the entire area, and, for the first time, heating to the workshops. This scheme was entered for the 1992 Gas

Energy Management Awards and the museum now proudly displays its winner's plaque in the foyer. It is easy to examine each energy-conservation measure in Table 1. The installation of the BEMS is discussed elsewhere and is therefore not shown on the Table.

Maintenance

It is reasonable to say that none of the schemes described was undertaken without first ensuring the plant was running to its designed specification. No energy-saving scheme will produce results without a thorough knowledge of the plant's capabilities and shortcomings. For instance, little would be gained by the purchase and installation of a variable frequency inverter to control the fan motor of an air-handling unit, if the unit could not cope with the demand in the first place.

Early schemes at the NMPFT addressed plant shortcomings and improved performance where possible, but, of course, an increase in power consumption was often inevitable. The humidification capacity of the main gallery air-handling unit has increased by over 500% or 54 kW!

Cooling/de-humidification capacity has likewise increased by over 500% so the continuing trend of falling fuel costs are of greater significance.

What next?

The next big push is to investigate all electrical motors, some of which are greatly oversized. Some would benefit from being converted to dual speed to cope with the different loads which occur during public hours and out of public hours.

Gallery lighting is also high on the list and a joint Estates/Curatorial team is investigating new energy-efficiency schemes for introduction at gallery refurbishment time. On the list of desirables would be a gas-driven chiller, which would produce additional cooling more cheaply whilst at the same time providing valuable DHW as a 'free' by-product. The museum is currently in the process of concluding an agreement with British Gas to install such a chiller on a two-year field trial, which, if successful, would give the museum an option to purchase at a significantly reduced cost, if the desired performance and savings are achieved.

Finally the wheel comes full circle. The museum is about to enter negotiations with alternative suppliers of energy as existing contracts run out and the minimum supply thresholds of National Power and the like fall below the 500 KVA limit.

This brings the museum to 1993 when other areas, such as the extension of air-conditioning, will be considered. In the meantime, the energy-efficiency programme will tick over, waiting for new technology to catch up.

The environment post modernisations

The museum is now able to achieve the desired environmental conditions under all but the most extreme conditions. The BEMS allows the flexibility to alter conditions instantly gallery by gallery, thus saving energy when non-sensitivel collections are being displayed. Environmental conditions are now continuously monitored and the facility now exists which allows an instant response to a BEMS-generated alarm indicating either plant breakdown or climatical conditions outside preset limits. The BEMS datalogging system is starting to replace the use of thermohydrographs, by producing graphs of gallery conditions and summaries of data for both the curator and the engineer.

The building energy-management system

Four years ago the response time to a breakdown of critical equipment could be weeks, due solely to the complex and fragmented nature of the services. Now response is immediate. The value of immediate response can never be truly measured since the cost to the collections of time spent in unsuitable conditions cannot be measured.

What can be measured is the marked improvement in environmental conditions and the dramatic financial savings realised on energy. The BEMS now gives the museum the ability to monitor constantly, record conditions, breakdowns, usage and energy consumption and to react accordingly at the push of a button.

The basic supply and installation of the first outstation and operator's panel cost £9,000. This installation addressed major deficiencies in the air-conditioning systems of the main display galleries. Since 1988 no further capital allocations have been made available, but the museum has made a commitment to reinvest all savings into further energy-conservation measures. It is difficult to assess fully the cost, however the installation which now comprises of nine outstations, each with approximately 100 control or monitoring points, replacement actuators for valves and dampers, replacement temperature and humidity detectors, the latest personal computer with colour monitor and the latest colour graphics printer, has cost in the region of £55,000. In-house electricians have installed over 6 miles of screened data cable, contactors, relays and new electrical distribution boards to accommodate new controls and provide a higher degree of control of lighting and power circuits.

123

The BEMS's ability to switch off and on gallery lighting not only saves energy, but frees the time of the gallery curator who is no longer required to carry out morning and evening lighting rounds. It is fair to say that many of the schemes outlined in Table 1 were made possible by the flexibility of the BEMS. The facility to write programmable points whereby many control parameters are able to cross-reference one another is a crucial feature in establishing a balance between energy conservation and the environmental conditions of the museum. Therefore energy-saving schemes can be overridden as soon as gallery conditions move outside preset tolerances.

The system also permits easy and rapid access to change control parameters and timings in the event of holiday periods, special events, or even the museum having particular sensitive parts of the collections on display.

The savings generated by the energy-conservation measure amount to over 40% of the museum's 1988 budget allocation. With the aid of the BEMS, the next decade will bring on-line full condition-based maintenance management. This way maintenance tasks will only be scheduled after a signal from the BEMS to the linked asset management system indicating breakdown, plant performance monitoring or hours run. This is likely to provide significant savings in maintenance costs and a far higher degree of budgetary control.

Biography

Tim Whitehouse apprenticed as a Marine Engineer for 6 years in the Royal Navy before taking up employment with a number of HVAC companies. He gained qualifications in building services engineering and in 1985 gained a Diploma in Energy Management at Portsmouth Polytechnic before joining Norfolk County Council as engineer responsible for all council-owned buildings in the South Norfolk area. These included the Castle Museum in Norwich and Norwich City College where he was appointed Chief Engineer and part-time lecturer in heating technology to City and Guilds students. In 1987, after a move to South Norfolk District Council as Senior Services engineer, he won the British Gas Award for an innovative scheme which cut energy bills by over 40% in a home for the elderly. In 1988, he moved to Bradford, where he joined the National Museum of Photography, Film and Television as Building Services Manager. After five years he left the museum to join the BBC where he is responsible for services to over seventy Northern Region properties and a member of the BBC's Environmental Steering Group.

Table 1 Major energy-saving schemes.

Year	Scheme	Benefits	Cost	Payback	Annual Saving
1988	Replace/convert ceiling lighting on foyer and stairs area from 120W tungsten to compact fluorescent.	Reduced maintenance, over 80% saving in energy.	£3000	0.4 Year	£7500
1988	Fit compensated controller, time clock, motorized valve and indirect cylinder to Admin area heating system.	More comfortable office temperatures, night set back of temps, significantly cheaper DHW costs.	£1800	0.5 Year	£3600
1988*	Motorized dampers on Kodak AHU and provide enthalpy programme.	Free cooling and improved environmental conditions.	£1500	0.6 Year	£2500
1988	Provision of power factor correction equipment to incoming electrical supply.	Large savings on electrical costs.	£1500	1½ Years	£10000
1989*	Fit recirc ducting and motorized dampers to Airedale AHU and enthalpy programme.	Free cooling and improved environmental conditions.	£5000	1 Year	£5000
1989	Fit time clocks and contractors to Kodak Lighting. (Enabling later connection to BEMS).	'ON' periods restricted to opening hours rather than when the duty curator does his/her rounds.	£2000	1 Year	£2000
1989	Fit fluorescent lights to gallery for cleaning.	Reduction of power costs extension of display lamp life.	£1500	0.5 Year	£3000
1989*	Fit recirc ductwork and motorized dampers to Imax and multi media projection box AHU's.	Free cooling and improved environmental conditions.	£5000	1 Year	£5000
1990	Fit solenoid valves controlled by occupancy detectors to automatic cisterns, cistern dams to W.C., non concussive taps. Lighting also linked into PIR detector.	40% reduction in water costs and small reduction in lighting and flushing costs.	£4000	0.4 Year	£5000
1990	Negotiate reduction in gas tariff.	Approx. 8% reduction in gas charges.	NIL	NIL	£1300

Year	Scheme	Benefits	Cost	Payback	Annual Saving
1990	Fit solenoid valve to Imax air compressor cooling water supply linked to open only when motor is running.	Over 70% reduction in water consumption of compressor.	£250	0.9 Year	£300
1990*	Remove two vast horizontal D.H.W. calorifiers, replace with a vertical direct fired gas calorifiers.	a) Reduction in risk associated with legionnaires disease. b) Permits main boiler plant to be shut down in summer. c) Significantly more efficient operation.	£5000	1.3 Years	£3000
1991	Provide gas supply to Kodak Museum extension, removal of 36 KW electric boiler providing heat to constant temperature circuit. Removal of 6 × 3 KW over sink electric DHW heaters, replace with 2 × 18 KW condensing boilers an indirect cylinder.	Reduction of electrical demand over 50KW.	£8500	1 Year	£8500
1991	Fit new electrical meters with pulse counting.	Load shedding to auto consumption facility for pulse monitoring.	NIL	NIL	£2500 (Reduction in maximum demand charges)
1991	Consolidate electrical supplies disconnection 2nd supply by connecting the area to the main incoming supply, fed by a 11 KV transformer.	Reduction of costs by: a) Cheaper unit rate off main transformer. b) Elimination of 2nd standing charge.	£1000	3 years	£330
1992	Fit variable speed drives to main gallery air handling unit. Controlled via BMS to vary speed as dictated by internal conditions.	Reduction of costs by: 20% reduction in motor speed equates to 50% reduction in operating costs. Costs further reduced by eliminating the need to condition air excess to requirements.	£4000	1.3 years	£3000
1992	Fit dual speed motors to Kodak air handling unit.	Motor electrical load switches between 18KW and 2.5KW depending on demand.	£4000	1.3 years	£3000

*Linked to BEMS during conversion to provide control and energy-saving programmes.

Management Priorities for Environmental Control and Energy-Efficient Practice in Museums

May Cassar MSc FIIC The Conservation Unit, Museums & Galleries Commission

These rules of thumb are offered to help develop good practice in environmental control and energy efficiency or to review existing practice when:

    i. planning a new building.

    ii. renovating an existing building.

    iii. installing new environmental control equipment.

    iv. upgrading existing environmental control equipment.

In all of these areas *good design, careful execution and competent management* are required in order to realise worthwhile benefits.

1. Do simple things first:

When planning a new building, be prepared to ask for low-energy features. They are often simple and straightforward!

Before renovating an existing building, find out how energy is being used and identify where energy-savings can be made. You may find that the priorities are not quite what you thought!

2. Adapt the appropriate Standards, Codes and Guidelines to your particular situation:

Do not adopt published recommendations wholesale. Accept that in the interest of energy efficiency, the building can be allowed to ride seasonal fluctuations without putting the collection at risk, by permitting a gentle drift between summer and winter temperature and humidity conditions.

3. Carry out energy-efficiency improvements thoroughly:

It is important to look not only at upgrading equipment with more energy-efficient appliances, but also at whether building improvements can exploit rather than replace intrinsic low-energy features in the original building. Retain and develop the good features, such as wooden window shutters, and eliminate or minimise the bad ones, such as large areas of single-glazing.

A significant reduction in energy costs is usually possible if better equipment and controls are accompanied by improvements to the building's air-tightness, glazing and insulation.

Be aware that improvements to the fabric may give disappointing results if services and controls are not altered (or at least adjusted accordingly).

In new services design, consider ducting conditioned air from areas needing high-quality control to areas that can make do with a less stringent specification. For example, from air-conditioned galleries and stores to public spaces.

4. Consider the various uses of space within the building:

By moving different functions around, advantage can be taken of the natural environmental characteristics of the building and reduce lighting, heating/cooling and ventilation loads.

For example, collections in storage do not require daylight or natural ventilation, while occupants of a building do. Therefore, it makes sense to place people near the perimeter of the building, while collections are housed more centrally.

5. Use appropriate technology to service the building:

Building services should be installed and operated in harmony with the building as a whole. For example, excess heat should be exhausted or redistributed rather than fighting it with refrigeration.

For the most reliable results, advanced technology should be used as a direct replacement for conventional technology. For example, condensing boilers should be used as a direct replacement for conventional boilers and high-frequency light fittings should replace low-frequency light fittings.

It is worth remembering that, where possible, the installation of intrinsically efficient appliances is usually preferable to new pieces of equipment being added to improve to old technology.

6. Operate and control environmental equipment effectively:

A control system must not be so complex that the museum is unable to operate the equipment with the skills available to it in house. The importance of training and discussion are vital to ensure that everyone knows how the controls are supposed to work and what the reporting lines are in case of failure.

Sub-metering can be useful in specific areas, such as the restaurant and for energy-intensive items of equipment, such as fans and steam humidifiers. This gives management information on running costs of different areas and particular items of equipment. The status of equipment and alarm conditions should also be clearly indicated.

It has been stated that 20% of the effort produces 80% of the results. Therefore it is better to ensure that high-priority measures are done well and avoid a mass of marginal features that only give the appearance of improvements.

However, none of these measures will make a significant impact on the operating costs of a building if they are carried out in isolation, outside a management framework. For cost-effective improvements, determination to carry these measures through must exist within the senior management structure of the museum.

Biography

May Cassar is a Conservator and an Environmental Engineer. She has studied at the Institute of Archaeology and at the Bartlett School of Architecture, both part of University College London. She has been employed as Environmental Adviser at the Museums & Galleries Commission (MGC) for the last five years, initially to write a book titled, 'Environmental Management: Guidelines for Museums and Galleries', to be published in 1994. Recently she has been advising museums and galleries on environmental improvements in connection with the provision of appropriate environments for collections in new and refurbished buildings. She has also managed a number of projects for the MGC including: a study on the environmental performance of display cases, a survey of energy-use in museums and galleries, an evaluation of electronic hygrometers and the production of a guide on the use by museums of industrial buildings. She has published widely and lectures both in the UK and abroad.

Selected References

Ambrosino P.E., 'Energy Conservation at the Cooper-Hewitt Museum: Renovation for Improved Mechanical System Efficiency' in *Technology and Conservation*, Boston, Spring 1976.

Burton R., *A Client's Energy and Environment Briefing Guide*, Energy Group North West, RIBA, CIBSE, RICS and CIOB.

CIBSE, *Building Energy Code*, Part 1: Energy Conserving Design of Buildings and Services, 1977; Part 2 (a): Calculating of Energy Demands and Targets for New Buildings, 1981; Part 3: Energy Conserving Operation of Buildings and Services, 1979; Part 4: Measurement of Energy Consumption and Targets for Existing Buildings, 1982.

CIBSE, *Guide to Energy Audits and Surveys*.

CIBSE, *Lighting for Museums and Art Galleries*, Lighting Guide: LG8, 1994.

CIBSE, *CIBSE Guide*, Volume A: Design Data: Volume B: Installation and Equipment Data: Volume C: Reference Data, 1986.

Energy Efficiency Office, *Introduction to Energy Efficiency in Museums, Galleries, Libraries and Churches*, 1994.

Department of the Environment and The Welsh Office, *The Building Regulations 1985. Conservation of Fuel and Power*, Approved Document L1, 1990 edition, HMSO.

Dirksen P.C., 'Gas Total Energy Case History: Worcester, Massachusetts, Science Center', in *Ashrae Journal*, Volume 15, No. 4, April 1973.

Kwok K. and Sinclair K., 'High Performance Energy Management at the Vancouver Art Gallery Brought Energy Costs Down and Provided Payback in Less Than a Year' in *Ashrae Journal*, May 1989.

Matthai R.A., 'Energy Conservation and Management: A Critical Challenge for Cultural Institutions' in *Technology and Conservation*, Boston, Spring 1978.

Matthai R.A., 'Reprise of a Crisis', in *Museum News*, Special Section: 1991 Annual Meeting, May/June 1991.

Miller H., 'Energy Conservation and Historic Sites: Old Buildings, New Tools', in *Energy Ideas*, US National Recreation and Park Association, Washington DC, January-February 1978.

National Trust for Historic Preservation, *New Energy from Old Buildings*, Preservation Press, Washington DC, 1981.

Reading A., 'A Control Philosophy for the Economical Air Conditioning of Museums and Galleries' in *Building Services Engineering Research and Technology*, Volume 4, No. 3, 1983.

Ucar M. and Doering G.C., 'Energy Conservation in Museums and Historic Buildings' in *Ashrae Journal*, Volume 25, No.8, August 1983.

Printed in the United Kingdom for HMSO
Dd296628 7/94 C12 G559 10170